Fifty Years in a Jealous Marriage

Seeking a Healthy Sexuality in a World of Power and Control

Reverend James Lex, Ed.D.
with Ann M. Ennis

CSS Publishing Company, Inc., Lima, Ohio

FIFTY YEARS IN A JEALOUS MARRIAGE
SEEKING A HEALTHY SEXUALITY IN A WORLD OF POWER AND CONTROL

FIRST CSS PUBLISHING EDITION
Copyright © 2003 by
Ann Ennis

Library of Congress Catalog Card Number: 2002108242

Editor: Fredrik Liljeblad, San Diego, California

While events really occurred, we have changed names
on a few occasions to respect privacy of those involved.

ISBN 0-7880-2061-7
PRINTED IN U.S.A.

*To honor all priests
who struggle with, yet love,
the Universal Church.*

Table of Contents

Introduction

I am a priest. I have been married for 50 years. That might sound sort of funny at first, but it does feel as if the Church and I have been married all these years. It's been an interesting and varied romance. The Church has had its ups and downs—and so have I. The Church has changed—and so have I. Sometimes we even changed together.

The Church changed in some ways that I was happy about. You don't get married expecting the other to change, but when it happens for the better—well, it's a good thing. Like a wife who changes and grows—it helps both of you get along better, and you are glad that she is happier. That's the way it was with the Church and me.

Sometimes the Church did dumb things, like force a lot of my priest friends out of the priesthood. And sometimes the Church hurt people. She has a habit of not really listening, and then arbitrarily making rules about people and their lives. My spouse can be insensitive at times. We have had a rocky romance, even though I lived with her for 12 years before we got married. Then I took the plunge. It has indeed been for better or worse, for richer or poorer, in sickness and in health, till death do us part.

In the first part of my life, marriage wasn't difficult. I was in love with her (the Church)—did all the right things, helped people. She reinforced my behavior. She told me I was good and that people were pleased. I was a good provider: I brought people into the Church. But if I did the least thing wrong, she had a great gift of making me feel guilty. That was her power—being able to beat me down with even the slightest provocation. She kept me in line during the first section of my life. But I thought it was a great marriage for about the first 15 years.

Then I got tired of her. I wanted to sow my wild oats and be on my own. In the second stage of my life, she got very jealous— maybe for good reason. She sent her friends to tell me "Stop that," "You can't do that," "A good priest is not supposed to do that." She had boosters. She tried to make me feel guilty like before, but it had less and less effect. Nevertheless, I stayed connected and close to her. We held on to our foundation of relationship. But I drifted. I stepped out of line. I did things that she was not proud of. And she let me know it. She even smacked me around a little. But we survived together. We never divorced. We never even truly separated, although we lived separate lives for a time.

I know I always loved her. I always kept coming back—as she knew I would.

In the third stage of my life, I settled down and directed more attention to the marriage. She gave me more freedom, while still being there for me—waiting patiently. She let me have my fun and roam and retire. She even helped provide for me in my retirement. I tried to keep up my side as well. I still love her.

I have to say that she did not want me to write this book. She is much more secretive than I, and much more for keeping secrets in the family. As for me, I have a strong need to share my 50 years of married life. She might have some problems with this now, but in the long run I know she will see that it is for the best. This book is part of what I had to do to live out my life and to share with others who I am.

As you read this book, look upon it as a struggle: Fifty years of married life to a jealous woman—the Church.

James Lex
September, 2001

Part I

Chapter 1
Learning the Code

I wish I could remember my big brother. He burned to death when he was four. I was two then. They told me that I was the one who found him burning near the kerosene heater in the bedroom. I pushed him into the family room, where my nearly deaf grandmother sat. He died two weeks later. It was 1927, and as Number Two son I had big shoes to fill.

All I ever heard was that my brother was a perfect angel. They called him "Billy Boy." He was named after my father, William Lex. Later in my life, my mother told me that at Billy Boy's funeral everyone said it was a shame the other one, the little moon-faced one—referring to me—hadn't been taken. My mother said, "I guess God left you here for a purpose." She really believed that. I never did until recently.

Once past my brother's death, and to the point where I can begin to remember my early years, I felt we had a nice enough life. Although I was born in Texas, we moved to southern Indiana after I was born to be near my father's family and the new family business, Lex Company Welding Supply. I had two sisters: Dorothy and Mary, born in 1927 and 1931, respectively; a younger brother, Robert, was born in 1929.

My family lived in a comfortable home near the center of Evansville, Indiana. Our home, with its bungalow-style accents and huge front porch, was on Franklin Street—part of a heavily German Catholic area two blocks off of Main Street. Ours was the only home with a driveway—*and* a car to go with it. My parents slept downstairs and we kids were packed into the upstairs loft room like residents in a dormitory. We considered ourselves poor, but so did everyone else in those days of the Depression. It was a simple time with few longings for luxury. My father now owned a welding supply business and warehouse. The Lex's—my parents, sisters, brother, and me—were doing just fine. I filled the eldest brother

9

role well. I walked to kindergarten by myself the first day and took my immunization shots without tears. Those were easy ones. Other incidents caused more pain.

I have only a few clear memories of my father. He was strong, had a good sense of humor, and a small streak of recklessness. One memory I have is of him buying liquor during Prohibition. Bootleggers would deliver it to us at night. Then he'd store it in the basement—that's where he drank it, too. I recall one Christmas that the two of us secretly dropped off a case of beer to the nuns at St. Joseph's Parish and then went home. When we got home, we called on the phone and whispered, "Present on your back porch," and then hung up like superspies. They knew it was Daddy and me. But it was fun to act like Santa.

Daddy died suddenly when I was eight. At that time, Dorothy was six, Bob was four, and Mary was two. Now my mother was alone. She went into shock. Her own father had committed suicide. Her eldest son—her firstborn—had died in a horrible way. Now her husband was gone and had left her with four kids, a pile of broken dreams, and lots of memories.

An avid and driven athlete, my father played tennis and handball often. After a handball game early one evening, he came home and collapsed in the bathroom. When Dorothy found him, he was already dead. It was a blood clot that had gone to his heart. They thought he had gotten hit while playing handball and that might have caused it. I remember Dorothy running toward me while I was out playing ball. It must have taken her a while to find me because, by the time we got back home, the body was gone. Daddy was 35. It was May, 1934.

They brought Daddy home for the wake. He was laid out in the front room with a mesh covering the open coffin. I recall my mother raising the mesh and kissing him. I thought that was odd: to kiss my father when he was dead. The adults left for the funeral, leaving us four kids behind with a family friend. We were taken for candy to distract us while the adults went to bury my father. People still do that today—"protect" kids from funerals. I wish I'd been allowed to go to Daddy's.

We got back home from the candy store about the same time as mother arrived from the funeral. And we all went to bed. In those days you didn't go to grief therapy. You didn't examine your feelings. You struggled and got on with it. The next morning we woke up and life went on. Except my maternal grandmother came to live with us. From a child's point-of-view, that was the worst of it.

My grandmother, Sarah McGrath Bianchi, was a typical lace-curtain, shanty Irish lady who couldn't trust anyone. She worried constantly about how we looked and what people thought of us. I don't know how mother put up with her. My grandmother controlled things—everything. Mother, who was supporting her in every aspect of life, had to hide personal purchases from her. My grandmother wouldn't allow mother to have anything nice and new.

We kids thought Grandmother hated us, but she was probably trying to motivate us the best she knew how. Still, it hurt deeply, and does even now. My grandmother always wanted to protect us from the sin of vanity. If we got a good grade in school, or if an endeavor went halfway well, she undercut it and told us not to become proud. Mother taught us manners and respect—even respect for my grandmother. What my grandmother taught us was to be nervous and untrusting of ourselves.

A lot of my hang-ups came from her, especially my concern with other people's opinions of me and my low self-esteem. My grandmother had no self-esteem and she tried to push that onto everybody else. Her Italian-American husband, my grandfather, had killed himself and even to this day I am sure she somehow drove him to it. She couldn't help it. It was her nature. Her son, my Uncle John, would have nothing to do with her. That is why she came to live with us. It really had little to do with my father's death. That was just the excuse—or the opening of a space. Yet she was well liked in the neighborhood. In public, my grandmother was a great sport and everyone outside the house thought a lot of her. She lived with us from the time we were young until her death. She was only around 60 when she moved in. She lived to be 99.

Mother threw herself into the work and the family—running the house like a branch of the business. She loved us and took great

11

care of us, but she almost never *touched* us. The fear that she might lose another one like she lost her first child kept her distant in many ways when we were kids. But she was fun, always fun. My grandmother was our stereotypical mean-old-mother. And my mother loved fun; she was a frivolous big sister who would sneak off and treat us to ice cream. We laughed a lot, even if we weren't caressed.

We all knew about our grandmother, too. We talked openly about her, telling our mother to kick her out. "Get rid of her," we'd beg. "But she's my mother and she has no place else to go," she would answer. "Uncle John doesn't want her. We have to do it." That sense of obligation, of constantly striving to do the "right thing" 100 percent of the time. A soft touch, that was my mother.

Mother dated several different men, but the four of us and our clever little antics kept her from getting serious. But then, perhaps she never wanted to get serious in another relationship—because of what she had been through. She was probably terrified of love.

So by the time I was eight, I had lost a brother and my father. I had a cruel grandmother in the house. It was the Depression. You grew stoic very quickly in those times. The Church was a strong and flowing undercurrent in our lives—St. Joseph's Roman Catholic Church. It stood down the street, solid and huge, with brown brick walls and green tile roof. It was there for the funerals. It was there for the Sunday Mass that we kids couldn't fathom. It was there, near the school—like the trees, the coal dust, and the wind in our lives.

Church, for a Catholic child in those days, meant the Sisters. Your interaction with the nuns was much more real than the mystery of a Latin Mass. The Sisters of St. Benedict taught at St. Joseph's Parish School. They were great and seemingly normal—most were young, but not all. They blended together because their habits hid nearly every feature. Sisters were gender-neutral. Nice, wise creatures, they molded us much more than the priest ever did.

Away from the school, icons of Catholic culture filled our home—crosses, holy cards, statues. It was normal and a part of the natural way of life for us. The neighbors were Catholic, too. Evansville itself was 25 percent Catholic. Vigil candles and rosaries were the stuff of daily life. We Catholics were normal, the community's leaders.

In school, we had Mass daily, but not daily Eucharist. To take Eucharist you had to make a confession. We only made a confession on the Thursday before First Friday—the first Friday of each month. These confessions were ritual formalities. A game we played for our teachers and parents. We each had our own system. For example, everything I did, I did three times. So at confession it would be, "I fought with my brother three times." "Say three Our Fathers." The next time it was, "I was disrespectful to my mother three times." "Say three Hail Mary's." Then on the next morning, it being First Friday, we fasted before Mass. All the rules being fulfilled, we could have Communion. But after Mass, and this was the joy of it, we'd get free chocolate milk and sweet rolls in class. Well, maybe they charged us a nickel. But that made First Fridays really special.

Obviously, my prayer life was rather shallow. Prayer seemed sissy to me. For the non-sissy, there were sports. Alongside the Roman Catholic Church, ever-present in my life, were sports: kick ball, stickball, baseball, basketball, football, even some boxing. Sports. Now *that* was something to get excited about! There was my spirituality.

I remember playing baseball in the alley behind our home. First base was a telephone pole, second was a brick in the center of the alley, and third was another pole. The whole field was maybe 30 feet wide. It was great. In addition to the alley, we often played in the school lot. On the baseball field of St. Joseph's School, I met the first priest I ever liked. Young, tall, and muscular, Father Leonard came over and played ball with us occasionally. The first time he ever did, he hit that ball for an outright, real live, home run—one even a team of adults couldn't have fielded. I was impressed.

13

Chapter 2
Learning the Trade

It was at the end of seventh grade that Ed, a neighbor down the block, invited me to come up and take a tour of St. Meinrad Seminary. Ed, age 14, was in his first year of study at St. Meinrad. He thought I might enjoy life there. The seminary was connected to a Benedictine Monastery about 50 miles from my home. St. Meinrad was a fortress of sandstone above the town of the same name. The small village was the abbey, more or less. The abbey, college and monastery dominated this beautiful hill far into the country. It looked like a castle to my city boy eyes. The tall sandstone spires, the timeless permanence of the adjacent buildings, the surrounding trees. There were no women—no mothers, sisters, grandmothers— exotic living at its best. To top it all off, there was a real baseball diamond, a real football field, and real inside basketball courts. No more alleys, telephone poles, or bricks. Just guys and sports and this idyllic setting. I was sold.

Sixty years ago, it was not abnormal for a Catholic boy—especially one from a large family—to attend prep school at a monastery. It got him away from his family's fussing and the single bathroom. It had independence written all over it. So, when Ed invited me to visit, I took the offer. My idea was not necessarily to become a priest. I was 12 and ready to get out of the house, far away from all the chaos. I think I was also anxious to get away from all the work I was doing. I could see that the guys at St. Meinrad thoroughly enjoyed themselves. My major and most lasting impression of the atmosphere not surprisingly revolved mostly around all these guys playing ball. At St. Meinrad, as opposed to St. Joseph's in Evansville, each class held 30 or 40 students—all male of course— as well as the entire school staff. That didn't bother me then—or at any time in seminary. Also, the school intramural squads featured a number of teams. I was ready to go so I could play ball.

The next year, 1938, I would please a lot of people by going away to seminary. Entering the seminary was no small thing. The neighbors and my mother thought it was really something. Sending a young boy to the seminary was a source of neighborhood pride in those days—every bit a great thing. All Catholic families wanted a priest. Everyone loved it when they got one. My eighth grade class at St. Joseph's Parish School, and the class immediately preceding it, produced five priests. Although priesthood wasn't the goal, I just naturally fell into it.

In my young mind, the seminary was a win-win situation for us all: Mother would be proud; I would gain independence; I would get out of that house full of women. I was ready to go. My eagerness thus indicated, it was decided that I would go after completing eighth grade. The sisters at St. Joseph's may also have been grooming me for the priesthood a bit. Looking back, I feel that they wanted me to become a priest. At every chance in school, they encouraged me to take on leadership, and so I did—to make them happy. I was not a good student, but I was active and well liked.

The next year of school, in eighth grade, I was able to become captain of the safety patrol sponsored by the American Automobile Association (AAA). AAA provided flags, hats, and badges. We stood on the street corners and helped children get home from school safely. The sisters pushed me a little into this job. The safety patrol was looked up to with respect. I enjoyed being in charge. Looking out for others' safety, blowing whistles, telling people what to do—perhaps I really could be a priest. Priests wore uniforms and thought they were in charge, too.

Not long after my visit to St. Meinrad, I went to tell our pastor, Father Michael, of my holy intentions. I rang his front bell. "What do *you* want?" came the booming, irritated voice from behind the door. "I...I want to go to St. Meinrad..." I fairly shook in replying to the priest. "Oh, well, come right in my son." I should have gotten a hint. What did this change in reception imply about these guys? Were they irritable and high strung? I didn't catch on until later.

While I didn't understand Father Michael, I thought tall, strong, baseball-hitting Father Leonard was...well...super. He was a great guy. He was an athlete. Everyone liked him. Ever since that day on the field at school, I thought, "Boy, I want to be like him." Father Leonard represented what I thought being a priest would be: respect and athletics. Father Leonard was a gem. He helped me a lot

15

later on, after my ordination, when I was assigned to be associate pastor for a paranoid hypochondriac—but that story comes later.

I was 13 when I left for St. Meinrad. From that time on, I was only with men. I went from a household of women to a community of men. Seminary in those days set adolescents directly on the road to becoming a father—*the* Father. The administration didn't mince words or waste time. On a student's first day, the administration gave each boy a cassock and collar. We were pubescent miniature priests.

Ed continued to support me for that first year. Although he was unlike my heroes of the time, more artsy and not at all athletic, he prevented the older guys from "scooping" me too much. Scooping was like hazing; they scooped a newcomer up and carried him to the music room. As one guy belted out some song very loudly on the piano to hide the screams, the others all held the newcomer down and basically beat on his stomach until it was all red. Ed protected me. After my first year, though, I didn't see him much. I don't think I ever let him know how much I appreciated his help. He died in an earthquake in the late 1950s as a missionary in Peru.

Scooping was the freshman hell, but for me so were the classes. At that time the school structure demanded a lot from students in the form of extreme mental pressure, but it was a college preparatory school, and a stable for grooming future priests, so that's not surprising. The schedule demanded first six years of religious-based high school with some college courses, followed by two more years of undergraduate college, then four years of graduate studies in theology. Twelve years, all of it expected to be in the same school, high on a green hill in southern Indiana.

For high school and college students, classes ran from 8:00 to 4:00, Monday through Saturday, except Tuesday and Thursday afternoons. These were free—for sports!

After seminary years, I tried hard to forget most of my teachers. The athletic priests—the coaches and the guys who excelled on the field—they were always my heroes. Father Dunston supervised the athletics. He didn't quite play with us the way Father Leonard had, but he had his fun. He was the kind of guy who would

16

pull a handkerchief from his cassock and his shorts would fall out. You knew he probably had his swimming suit on under the clothes.

The sense of community among students grew as new friendships formed. Although most were from southern Indiana, St. Meinrad had some guys from Louisville, Indianapolis, and eastern Indiana, too. We guys slept 40 to a dormitory room. Evening talk and antics compare to the best memories of summer camps. Tuition was $600 a year. The diocese paid in most cases, but my mother paid my way because we could afford it. I was happy enough at St. Meinrad, even though I was unsure whether I had a vocation or not. The community, with its openness and deep friendships, met my young needs. I enjoyed the sports, the fun, the doing, and the being. Seminary was a kind of cover for what was really an all male club—a good fraternity—that we belonged to. The studies were secondary. Ordination to the priesthood was 12 years away— a literal lifetime in my case.

I really got into the macho man bit—sports, football, baseball, everything. I was also at the center of things when it came to social events and parties. At St. Meinrad I led—not in the classroom, but socially and athletically. The school was the obstacle course: If I could get through it then I could be a priest and do these good things for people. That's what I thought it was all about.

From day one of the first class and for 12 years after, I learned to worry. Mostly I worried about grades. I have a report card that shows that at one time I was 38th out of a class of 38.

These cards were sent home, and my brother and sisters took great joy in telling everyone how dumb I was. That summer I went home to a new house. My family had moved from Franklin Street to Powell Avenue on the city's east side. My new parish for the summer would be St. Benedict's. After the first year and my first summer vacation, I returned to St. Meinrad for fall classes. One of the teaching priests asked me "What are you doing here? I thought you were going to quit." I think I stayed that year just to prove him wrong. The cycle of academic hell, athletic release, and summers home continued. Each summer was an escape from the labors of studying, which I traded for labors of a financial nature.

By June I'd go home and work. Most of the time I worked for the family business, Lex Company. I would load trucks with welding supplies for customers, the local industrial contractors. I would also unload or load boxcars for the warehousing part of the business. I recall working one hot August unloading a boxcar of linoleum by hand. I loved the demands for physical strength and stamina in the hot, humid Ohio Valley summers. I liked the work a lot and considered going into the business. It was ready-made. It would have been so simple. But somehow, I just never did.

In an attempt to develop this unformed vocation of mine, I tried to go to church every day during the summer. It was a little tricky. Because of my sweaty summer job, I usually wore old and very dirty clothes. The regular pastor had no problem with it. He understood where I was working and what I was trying to do. Once, though, there was a visiting priest who refused me Communion because I wasn't dressed properly. That really upset me. I vowed that I'd be a priest one day just to show people that not all priests were like this guy. Not all priests are arrogant and caught up in protocols. In a negative manner this visiting priest was a positive influence on me.

My goals changed dramatically from month to month in those years. First of all, going to seminary meant getting away from home, which was good. Then, once I had gotten away, the goal became to stay with the guys, my friends. But over the semesters, this or that guy left—departing seminary. Some of the ones who left were my best friends. With each departure, I thought I should also leave— but that would have taken nerve. Seminary was indoctrination. The teaching priests constantly talked about "your vocation." They gossiped about any boy or young man who quit. Rumors of his weaknesses, his real motives, his letting down his family trickled through the halls. I had to stay. Guys who quit during the 12 years found themselves shunned by their teachers, pastors and peers. It took great courage to leave.

Over time I began to believe that God wanted me to become a priest, just like the rector and teachers had said. Secretly, I didn't want to do it but I could not quit. I wanted to be thrust out. At night and in Vespers, I prayed that I would catch tuberculosis or that my fingers would be chopped off in an accident. These were considered impediments to ordination. Although I tried to talk myself into leaving, there was not a time or way to leave. So I stayed. It was one of those constant battles and I would inch along. I'd pray for a sign, but there never was one. "Well, God didn't give me a sign to leave, so I'll stay." Maybe that was the sign I'd been looking for.

Chapter 3
In Control

Seminary academics were complete hell. Maybe tuberculosis would not get me booted out, but an accumulation of F's would do the trick. Maybe the teachers would give up and just kick me out. If they would make the decision for me, then it wouldn't be my fault. But that never happened. Part of the struggle grew from my uncertainties about the exact nature of the job. At age 19, 25, and even 28, I still thought of the priesthood as a job: something to do to be important, and to provide me with food, shelter, and clothes.

I was pre-Vatican II by nearly 20 years; questions that simply couldn't be asked out loud plagued me. I thought too much. My thoughts, my need to understand, were what made school hell for me. If I questioned the wisdom of the Mass being said in Latin, I would have never said it out loud. Who was I to question or change what had always been? Here I was, well on my way to the sacrament of Holy Orders, and I had no real idea of what it meant to be Catholic.

I wasn't a Catholic then; I was a naïve, eager-to-please youngster. I converted to Catholicism late in life, relative to my ordination. Up until my middle years, I had no real understanding of the Church or a calling. I believe many of us in seminary didn't. At least we never talked about it. Among ourselves, away from school, we never examined our motives or our vocation. We mostly just did what we were told. I was never committed to the priesthood with the same emotion that I was committed to the St. Meinrad community and the male-to-male relationships. Nevertheless, I went on. Gradually, as I got closer to ordination, I came to fully believe that the priesthood would be a good place for me.

At home, during the summers of my early 20s, there were lots of women around. The girls of my adolescence became young women, my sisters' friends. They gave me lots of adulation. I always heard them saying, "All the great guys are going to be priests." I enjoyed flirting and horsing around, but I never saw myself getting married. I was cocky. I was very proud. But if I was going to quit, the girls weren't the reason or motivation. I was kind of a slow learner in regard to sexuality. I didn't catch on until it was too late. And I never even seriously thought about getting married until many, many years later. No, as long as the guys were there to be pals with—and God didn't give me a sign—it was worth staying with the program.

Another opportunity to leave seminary took shape as World War II spread to include the United States. It was 1942 and I was 18 years old. The Second World War was a big part of my life even though I didn't fight in it. All of my old friends and former neighbors signed up and left Evansville to fight. As a seminary student I wouldn't be drafted. We were all classified 4F—with the insane and incompetents. I believe the armed forces knew that one just didn't want too many chaplains: Too much forgiving isn't good for a war.

I really wanted to leave the seminary and go into the service, but I never did. Instead, I worried and held fast to my extreme patriotism during this "good" war. I wrote to my friends in the far reaches of the earth from my small desk in a dormitory at St. Meinrad; I wrote every week to encourage them. I prayed for them, too. One of them died. A couple became prisoners of war. It was very sad. I have always felt that I let my friends down—that I didn't do the right thing by staying in school and letting them join up. If I had quit to go to war, what would my life have been like? I think I'd probably have felt guilty either way.

After six years in minor seminary, I switched over to the Benedictine monastery to follow a few of my buddies who had moved in that direction. I entered the novitiate for six months under the tutelage of a strict and puritanical monk. He and I had difficulty from the first. Nevertheless, the Benedictine philosophy of hospitality and comradeship attracted me. I had no studies or tests while there. This freedom gave me time to think about what I wanted. The monastery was a blessing. My time there was a gift. It allowed me to make a major decision all by myself—to leave the monastery and return to the seminary.

Getting back into the seminary was a bit tricky. I had to get re-accepted by the bishop of the Diocese of Evansville and I had been anything but a good student before I left. On top of that, my bishop didn't care for the Benedictines. "Anyone stupid enough to have anything to do with the Benedictines doesn't belong in this diocese," he had been known to say. So he put me off and off and off. I even briefly considered going to Texas to complete my studies. Fortunately, my new pastor at St. Benedict's, Father Gabriel, talked to the bishop and got him to accept me on probation. It worked out. In 1945, I went back to finish studies in theology at St. Meinrad.

So I kept on. I didn't get tempted by women; didn't go off to war. I just muddled and mucked through, waiting for the preparation to end. But St. Meinrad still had challenges to offer. For once, academics held promise for me. In all of my studies at St. Meinrad, I found my academic sustenance that year from two teaching priests. These two philosophy professors challenged and pushed me, and always got in my face, asking "Why, why, why?" I kept right up with both of them. I didn't cry or panic. I was excited by the unanswerable questions, by the imponderables. The other teachers gave assignments and I did them by trying to give each teacher what he wanted. Where was the fun in that? Where was the thought? I enjoyed being toe-to-toe with my philosophy professors and their "Why, why, why?" They stretched and challenged my mind.

One of the spiritually saving features of the major seminary was Father Paschal. As my spiritual director, he helped me keep a balance in my life. Father Paschal was the one who drew me to a devotion of the Blessed Virgin in a way that later led to my feminist approach to life. Father Paschal taught me about letting go and using the example of Mary. I came to see Mary as a real person, out chasing flies off the food and washing the dishes. My devotion increased as I understood her human frailty and stoic attitude. Father Paschal was the first to teach me about turning my life over to God through Mary and letting go of worry. Mary became the mediatrix, mother, and companion for me in my journey.

Father Paschal took care of me, guided me. He would often warn me to be careful of the company I kept and what I got drawn into. He wasn't against the more progressive issues, but he wanted me to think clearly of the consequences of my choices. I appreciated that. He invited me once, for a means of spiritual direction, to write a personal essay. My title was, *What's the Truth About Seminary?* For the first time in my life, I wrote directly from the heart. The writing became much more than an assignment. I did an extraordinary bit of soul-searching. Using examples, I showed how the seminarians were using deception and words to beat the system. I illustrated how the teaching priests ran from our questions and avoided any open discussion. Upon turning the paper in, I hung around while he read it. He got scared. He said it was quite good. He graded it and gave it back on the spot, telling me to destroy it without letting anyone else read it. He felt what it said, although true, would present an obstacle to my ordination. No bishop would want a priest who thought like that. I still have it stuck somewhere in my boxes.

Under Paschel's guidance, I learned about printing and publishing. Father Paschal ran St. Meinrad's printing operation, Abbey Press. He turned a profit at the job, which was rare. The profit gave him power. He had great freedom in selecting what to publish and best of all, the bishop couldn't touch him. One of those other printing jobs led me to meet students who were in a group called Catholic Action. The members advocated on behalf of poverty issues. Catholic Action had a magazine that I eventually helped publish. I was almost kicked out of school for my involvement with them when the seminary's administrators labeled Catholic Action a Communist plot to take over the school. Many teaching priests feared any organization that wasn't either the Legion of Mary or a sports club.

Actually, the group *was* a little subversive in that we considered how we as students could help the seminary. We sought to make it a better place—make it over in our own image and likeness. Those in authority, who were not exactly in our image and likeness, got nervous and wrote to the bishop about my involvement. He wrote me a note that basically said, "Stop it or leave!" You could just hear him gritting his teeth as he signed the letter. Following on the heels of my foray into the Benedictines, this encounter opened a book of what would be a great history between the bishop and me.

Bishop Grimmelsman was the Diocese of Evansville's first bishop. He came to the newly founded diocese in 1945. Around 50 years old, he had served, feared by all I assume, as rector of the Josephinian Pontifical Seminary. Running a seminary, running a diocese—to him it was all the same. His attitude was, "The people are your students and you tell them what they need to know." As bishop, his basic plan was to have discipline. He knew everything and carried all the responsibility. His notion of the Roman Catholic Church was that of a pyramid with him as the local point man. He did everything exactly the way he was supposed to do it. He was precise. He followed the rules. We were his responsibility—a heavy cross for him to bear. He served in Evansville for 25 years. Once he gave up the job, he and I got along just beautifully. But in 1946 I never would have guessed it would come to that sort of tolerance.

I learned a lesson from Grimmy's reaction to my experimentation with Catholic Action. Despite Paschel and the Blessed Mother, I worried. Equally important, though, I also learned to look outside the cocoon. I can never forget that the same Church who brought Grimmy to me also brought Catholic Action. It's a beautiful and mysterious Church.

Seeking beauty and mystery, and with a sense of adventure and wanderlust, I spent a few summers at this time working in the Dakotas on Sioux Indian reservations. As with my mother, I strongly felt the call to be of service. Catholic Action awakened me to the desperate needs of the poor in and outside the USA. I went to a group of Native Americans to bring them hope. What I got for my piety was a hellish beating. It seems that the young Native American men—my peers—weren't exactly aware how needy they were or how great this white seminarian was. They hung out with me nevertheless, because I had a car and we had some fun. But one night, I mouthed off about what they should do to relieve their situation. They set me straight in a physical way. I learned a lot that night about prejudice and naïveté—mine. We ended the summer with friendship and respect for each other. I was grateful.

The Catholic missionaries in the Dakotas also taught me about marketing. Constantly desperate for funding the mission, they used every bad break as a way to send an appeal. Once a building caught fire. I was rushing to get hoses, buckets, and people. But the priest sent for a camera. "Have to get those terrible fire photos. When it comes to the poor, the public only responds to a crisis," he said.

As the summer wound down and Labor Day came, I'd have to go back up the hill to St. Meinrad. It no longer looked like Camelot to me. The worry, headaches, stomach cramps came back. Misery. At night I'd lie in bed and worry in circles, would I ever make it as a priest? If I did, how long was I going to last? How would I live when I quit? I became depressed at my prospects before I had even taken my vows.

Over time I adjusted. My essay for Paschel taught me not to get angry, because anger gets you nowhere. My experience with the bishop taught me not to expect much from others, because then you can avoid a lot of disappointment. Mother taught me that low expectations lessen the pain of life. My Native American friends taught me that I wasn't all that admired, even with my collar. From general seminary experiences I picked up traits of fierce independence—to stand on my own and not depend on anyone. These are painful and debilitating life lessons for the average person, but to a priest they are true and valuable assets. It's still a painful way to start your career—your vocation. Yet I don't believe for one minute that I was in the minority in this thinking in the seminaries of the Church of 1948, 1952, or even 1960. Still, most of us stayed.

We learned how to say Mass, but we didn't learn the sensitivity to make it truly meaningful. We learned rules, techniques, and tricks to getting it all in so we'd be accurate. We learned the important stuff about matter and form in the Mass. It was as if that's all there was to it: the Baltimore Catechism and the "matter and form" of Mass. "Keep your fingers together." "When you bow to the altar, your lips are to touch the altar." We actually had classes where we'd all be there at fake altars practicing saying Mass. The teacher would walk round with a ruler and whack us if we didn't bow low enough. We were 24-year-old men at the time. We learned to accept authority. Above all we learned that doing the job technically correct and doing what we were told to do was of prime importance. There was no emphasis on the pastoral. What authority told us was important became what we believed was important. Doing it correctly was our goal.

When we were just about to complete seminary and make preparations for ordination, each seminarian had to make this major final decision about whether he was willing to sign on for a life of celibacy. "Final" because, if you weren't going to be celibate, they couldn't ordain you, could they? I was 24 then. I barely thought about the celibacy question. Even with my private worries, the community of the seminary—of the other students, my friends—made the sacrifice look manageable. I thought the camaraderie would continue: sports, big groups of roving guys sharing laughs. I wasn't going to be alone.

I didn't even know what celibacy was. Our teachers didn't make a big deal out of it. It was just part of the job: male, Catholic, celibate. In those days no one discussed the serious side effects a celibate life brought upon you. The existence of alcoholic priests, irritated priests and eccentric priests was no different than the existence of the alcoholic baker or eccentric mechanic down the street. I never thought about sexuality in those days. I had enough other worries. And sex wasn't a preoccupation, because at the time my needs were pretty well met. I had no urging or any sense of push to have sexual relationships or any relationship of a deeper nature. I had had one girlfriend, for a summer, when I was 12.

So, I joined. I have often wondered if, knowing then what I know now, I would have done it. I went ahead and did it—and I never completely regretted it. Thus, when I was 25, I was ordained a Catholic priest in the Order of Melchizedek. The next part of my life would reflect all of this training and all that had gone before. With many reservations, Bishop Grimmelsman turned me loose on the diocese.

Chapter 4
Learning to Manipulate

My first job as a priest was not in a parish, but in the chancery office. I went straight to the top—I was a nice guy and the monsignor liked me. He thought I'd do well there. In 1950 I found myself working in Evansville, in a room on the first floor of the Bishop's House—which also served as the entire Catholic offices for the diocese. I may have been nice, athletic even, but what I couldn't do was take care of an office. They put me into record keeping, even though I wasn't organized and couldn't type. From day one, I found myself badly lost in trying to keep the diocese up to date. The other half of my job was the saving grace. As the monsignor's assistant, I took care of ministry at St. Mary's Hospital. I really liked that. I did well. I was a gregarious person. I'd talk to anyone. I cross-visited— even with the Protestants. Many priests of the day looked at hospital work as an obligation, but I saw it as an opportunity. Rather than just administering Communion and last rites, I talked and listened and didn't leave as fast as others would.

Everyone has a story to tell and I let the patients tell me theirs. Then the man in the next bed would begin to share. Because I was a priest, people tended to talk about church and God and religion. One of these conversations even led to an offer of a pastor's position at a Presbyterian church in a nearby town. During the hospital assignment, I worked just as I had been taught: I was very, very helpful. I made myself needed, liked, and respected. For the moment all my needs were being met. I was turning into a good priest. But just then the chancery office moved me.

From 1950 to 1951, I went to Celestine, Indiana. There I spent the time with Father Aloysius. It was a brief stay in a tiny village on the outer edges of the diocese. Father Aloysius really didn't need an assistant, except for someone to go to the store for him and look after him, or try to keep him grounded in reality. The evening after I arrived, I took a bath. The rectory had no shower. It was a Friday night, and I had just moved all my stuff in. I was dirty and sweaty. Bathing seemed sensible. On Saturday, I was out fooling around getting familiar with the parish, church and community. I got dirty again and decided I'd take another bath. Well, I got a knock on my door. Father Aloysius said, "There is a rule in the house that we take just one bath a week. You already took yours. So I'm shutting off the water." I tried to talk with him, "Excuse me, Father, but is there a problem with the water?" He said we had to be careful. He didn't want to run out of water. "And by the way, I have noticed that you flush the toilet, too." "Yes." I felt it coming. "Well, you should use the outhouse unless it's an emergency or at night." That was Father Aloysius.

This behavior was typical of that encountered by young assistants from the old pastors in those days. They were old bachelors. Luckily for my sanity, Father Leonard, the athletic baseball hero of my youth, was assigned to nearby Jasper. I would often go over to visit him in despair, "I cannot put up with this nut." "Oh yes, you can," Father Leonard would say. "He's just old and sad. He doesn't know about life and living. He needs you to soften those rough old edges of his." Father Leonard taught me to understand. It wasn't easy.

Father Aloysius was not healthy in any sense of the word. A hypochondriac, always worried about his stomach and intestinal tract. He didn't hesitate to share every symptom with whoever was nearby. Any time he heard about a new drug, he sent me to the drugstore to get it. I was embarrassed to ask. I always defensively told the clerks that it was not for me. It was terrible. Every day I had to go and get him some medicine he had heard of on the radio. He listened to a lot of radio. He also made me almost sick every morning over breakfast. He would take his cup of coffee, put a raw egg in it, then break up his toast and add it. Finally, he would slobber the mess down. Not surprisingly, I found many reasons to do jobs outside. Some parishioners and I managed to build a baseball field. We also cleaned up the grounds under Father Aloysius's irritated gaze. Even he got into it after a while, though. One afternoon, he mentioned that he'd like a new roof put on the outhouse. That was my big gift to St. Celestine's.

Just as abruptly as I arrived, I left. In early January, 1952, I was moved to St. Mary's Church in Evansville. I was given one day's notice to move. As a young priest who really thought he knew something, but also had pangs of mistrusting power in the Church, moving back to Evansville proved educational for me. The move was due to some rumored shenanigans among some of the priests in town. One was supposedly sexually involved with some children. Another was involved in a threatened public lawsuit. Father John, the pastor at St. Mary's, was supposedly having an affair with his organist. I don't know about the others, but the rumors about Father John were wrong. Anyhow, the chancery office rapidly re-arranged several parish pastors.

Father John was only one in a cast of many participating in this absurd drama. He was a kind old man with bad eyes, and he was being mysteriously accused of philandering. "We are going to get rid of him," the higher-ups in the chancery office told me. My role was supposed to be Father John's replacement. Others on staff set me straight. A Mrs. Sasse, the neighborhood zealot from across the street, ran the whole parish from caring for the vigil lights to sweeping the front steps. I remember she had made a personal vow to always wear purple—and she did. I suppose she thought God liked purple. Every day she found out what we did wrong and she let us know. We didn't close the doors. We didn't clean up. Jeesh! Still, she loved Father John and looked out for him.

Then there was the housekeeper, who also tried to run things. Another cast member was the organist, the one accused of carrying on with Father John. She had a really bad time of it. Everyone was trying to protect Father John and keep things going. It was all a can of worms, but it was fun for me. The accusations weren't really believed by the people in the chancery office. They just wanted to move their offices into the roomier St. Mary's location. Even worse was their plot to dissolve the parish and make it the bishop's office. All they needed was to get Father John out. I moved to St. Mary's for what was supposed to be two weeks. I stayed there three years. They never did close the parish.

That parish office generated anxiety like a storm generates lightning. St. Mary's was a war zone as the folks at the chancery office bombarded Father John. Accusations and counter accusations flew through downtown Evansville. Secret meetings and not-so-secret meetings took place. People chose up sides. Priests either ganged up on the bishop or Father John, whichever could get them further. It was my first taste of church politics. It was fascinating. I inconspicuously watched from the sidelines. I fought the powers-that-be vicariously, through Father John's fight. Finally the tide turned against the chancery office. By this time, most of the priests had encountered the bishop's wrath, and therefore came to enjoy bugging him. Supporting Father John and gossiping about the chancery office provided an excellent outlet for their irritation, the bishop being on one side and Father John on the other. Nothing ever happened. No one blinked. No one moved. Nothing changed. I enjoyed it all immensely.

The parish had routines as well. Someone had to keep it all running while Father John fought the war. I went to the parish school daily and taught. I said Mass. I gave instruction to lots and lots of people. And I tried to help the poor. To see them I could sit out front and look through the window. Across Cherry Street were three or four houses of prostitution. I used to watch the guys stroll by, get picked up and sneak around to the side doors. It was a fascinating neighborhood. As a young priest, I sympathized with the panhandlers' stories, but gradually became hardened to their tales of bad luck. Still, I always used to find some way to help: either I got them food or took them to a nearby restaurant. Sometimes I'd call and tell the restaurant owner that we were coming in and he'd feed us. The Rescue Mission was nearby, and panhandlers could usually get in for the night. The Mission was very cooperative.

The parish's St. Vincent de Paul Society was a great help to the poor, too. More and more poor came to the area all the time. As the nearby hospital bought up lots of property, the neighborhood grew poorer. Downtown pushed toward us and the area became very commercial. It was one of the oldest parishes, but it was undergoing a lot of changes at this time. From my perspective, St. Mary's melting pot was a great pot to start in.

Father John was the best pastor I ever had—*ever*. A very kind man, he profoundly influenced my life. His way of helping and teaching, without ever giving direct answers or advice, broadened me and gave me strength for the many struggles that lay ahead. He loved the Church and had the ability to ignore politics and to rise above it. That's the way he was. The bishop never liked him because he was smart. He'd speak up to the bishop if given a chance, and never ducked an argument. Bishop Grimmelsman couldn't handle that. Theirs was a never-ending feud.

I often asked Father John for advice; he would never give it. He'd just say, "What do I know. I've just been here 37 years. I don't know any more now than I did when I came." I thought, "Wow! What in the hell? Is that the way it's going to be for me?" Through his eyes, the future began to scare me. At the time I was still into the priesthood for camaraderie and fun. At St. Mary's I saw that not all priests were comrades. And it wasn't all fun. At this war-torn parish, I was in a position of duty and responsibility. I had to run things. Hell, I wasn't even supposed to be there.

The entire church scene was beginning to be tiresome and very routine to me as a young priest—Mass droning on and people murmuring in the pews. More than once I fell asleep while saying Mass: In the process of speaking the prayers I would chant myself to sleep with the rhythm of the Latin. When I snapped awake, I would look to see where my hands were. The position of my hands was the only way I could figure out my place in the book of Latin sounds. Confessions filled the weekends. People lined up from all over the city and I sat for hours listening. I became a confession robot. Insert a "Bless me Father for I have sinned." And you receive, "Your penance is blah, blah, blah." But that is all the people wanted back then. That was all we knew. It is so much better now. Yet, hearing those mounds and mounds of confessions taught me about sin: my sins.

I always had an abnormal fear of sin, especially sexual sins. These were stressed so much in the seminary. The morals textbook that dealt with the Ten Commandments was about two inches thick. An inch and three-quarters of that book had to do with one of the Commandments. Guess which one? That's how I was trained. The entire emphasis was to be careful of the sexual sins. It really did heighten my awareness of homosexuality, sins of touch, lust, and more. In the neighborhood of St. Mary's, I faced my fears and adjusted them. I lived in a neighborhood of sin. All day long on

Saturdays I listened to lists and lists of sins. I had prostitutes across the street. The chancery people coming to the rectory door were all liars. It was a menagerie of sin. What a way to start. What a great way to get educated about the bigger picture.

I remember the first time a person came to confession and said, "I am a homosexual." Whoa! I was caught. In a flash thoughts shot across my brain, "Who is this? Oh, it's him. Am I attracted to him? How? Am I homosexual?" His words made me examine my conscience. I felt much empathy for this man. In the mid-1950s that must have been an incredibly horrible thing for him to confront— and so honestly. "It's neat you came," I said. "It shows how hard you are struggling." That makes me cringe a little now. Nevertheless, I was a booster for him. I helped him make something good from his confession. And that's what it's really all been about— *always*.

Chapter 5
Always Outside the Group

St. Mary's Parish had lots of teenagers. As the young priest, I naturally fell into youth ministry. We had great fun in the mixed company of teenage girls and boys—a mixture I was never exposed to as a teenager myself. I was the group's Daddy, the Big Brother: the one with a car who could take them places. It was kind of odd, in a way. Looking back, though, my emotions were appropriate for the situation. I was balanced in my relations with the young group. We staged mini-dramas, took hikes in the county, and met with various other parish clubs. We hung around together at local church picnics, often went to Lincoln State Park, and I even put a rumble seat in my car so we could go as a big group. Together we built two youth centers for the group.

I felt needed and affirmed by the group and their parents. Even with the politics and covert dealings, life could still be fun. I met my needs through giving of myself to the larger community. I got energy from these surface relationships. The teens allowed me to feel needed. It was a terrific, energetic group of young people. We worked together; we played together.

I loved every one of them in a real sense—still keep in touch with many of them. Still, I didn't share myself with them. My age and role in the parish prevented it. I couldn't tell them about my own feelings. The youth group was the only organization with which I had a close relationship, yet I couldn't even talk openly with them. I had no one with whom to share my deepest feelings. This unbalanced reality carried over into my other work in the priesthood. I gave religious instruction to lots of people who were interested in becoming Roman Catholics and I found myself becoming overly attached to them. I enjoyed their coming over. I cleaned up and put on a little aftershave. I anticipated the sharing and the good feelings of being with people and being needed. I needed to be needed. Their adulation and affirmation was all I had.

One day, out of the blue, a letter came notifying me that I had been transferred to Sacred Heart Parish on Evansville's west side.

I had to report there the following Tuesday with all my posses-
sions. I was heartbroken, but I couldn't tell anyone how hurt I was.
I had to be strong and quiet. I had to be the priest as he is supposed
to be. It was sort of unhealthy.

Moving into Sacred Heart put me with a new pastor and another associate. The pastor was Monsignor Clark, who had for-
merly been my mentor and got me into the chancery office directly
after ordination. He, along with Monsignor Meyer, worked at the
chancery office. The business with Father John over my three years
there had discolored my trust of the chancery office more than a
little.

At Sacred Heart, I was really being taken advantage of in the
most passive sense of the phrase. The deal turned out to be that
Clark and Meyer would work at the chancery office, while I would
be doing the entire parish by myself. The Legion of Mary, St.
Vincent De Paul, Catholic Youth Organization, baptisms, funerals,
weddings, confessions, instruction, the school—all of it. It put me
to thinking: "Is this the way it works? Does God really want it to
be that the bishop can just stick us anywhere he wants us without
regard to our feelings?" I started doubting this whole concept of
God's will. Despite that, I got in there and did it.

As I had done at St. Mary's, I fell into working with young
couples and young people. We started a Christian Family Movement Group. We also expanded the youth group. Instead of just
one group, we had several smaller groups, based on age. It provided better contact with the teenagers and worked well. It also
entailed more responsibility on my part.

I remember creating a clubhouse in an old warehouse. We talked
the owner into letting us use the large room in the basement. We
remodeled it and put in studs for the walls, and electric wiring for
lights and such. The youth group liked being away from the parish
grounds. The warehouse was right in the heart of the west side. We
offered auto repair classes for the guys; girls had dancing and handi-
crafts. It was a great set up. But there were not too many chaperones. I have always been poor about getting chaperones. I trust
people—my romantic side, I guess. We had a rule: No beer. No
drinking on the site. One Sunday, I went down to the club and

34

found little black marks all over the walls. It looked like something had hit the wall repeatedly. Then I caught the old sewer smell of rotten beer.

I called the boys together later that day. They admitted to having a party on Saturday night. "Did you have beer?" "Yes." "Did you know that was wrong?" "Yes." "What are those black marks?" "Well, we got to drinking and then we started taking the records and sailing them at each other. They would hit the wall and break." They had destroyed hundreds of records. I was furious. But what a great story: all these drunk adolescents hurling 45s across the room all evening long. Nevertheless. "What do you think I should do about this?" The guys decided—on their own—that I should punish them by taking a belt to their rear ends as they leaned over the room's pool table. "Are you sure?" "Yes." "Well, how many times should I whack you?" "Maybe once for each bottle of beer we drank." "OK."

In the end, they came in one at a time, leaned over the table and said "Six." Six whacks. "Seven" Seven whacks. "Ten" Ten whacks. "Three." Three whacks. Then one boy, whose name I have forgotten, came in and said, "I didn't drink anything, but I would appreciate it if you would at least whack the table a couple of times so the guys won't think I'm a sissy." So I beat the table a bit and he went out feeling satisfied that the peer pressure was off and that he was one of the guys. The experience solidified our relationship so well that these people still seek me out—50 years later. In their eyes, I guess, I handled the situation well enough.

Inside the rectory, life had fewer rewards. Clark and Meyer left together every morning, came home from work and talked shop over dinner. I felt intentionally dealt out of the conversation. They lived their lives outside the parish. I was not really welcome in their circle. So I ate and went on to do my work running the parish. In spite of living with two priests from the chancery office, I liked the assignment.

I learned even more about Church politics, parish life, and children. I also learned some things about myself. I learned about personal, emotional pain. It hurt when my roommates ignored me. At times, dealing with the youth hurt because teenagers are always going to do something stupid to get them and me in trouble. I learned, like a parent learns, that you have to try to understand them, protect them, allow them independence and yet stay close by. Sacred Heart also provided me with lots of work to do in the community and parish. I blessed the new and exciting local TV stations. I gave retreats. People liked me, lots of people. So I got plenty of good ego stroking. It looked like I was one of the most successful priests.

What with the teenagers, priests, and ministry, I found myself having my own family. During these years, I had actually lost track of my real family's day-to-day life. The push and pull of my work kept me preoccupied. Mother and Bob were still running the family business; my sisters were both getting married, settling down, and having children. I was being "the good priest." Although I had inner doubts about my position in the Church, I talked vocations and gave instruction wholeheartedly. It was the thing to do. I rationally believed everything I taught or said, but I was also bored by it. I guess that this was probably typical. My emotional life was dead. In that situation, the Church doesn't excite you.

I was 30 then. I was doing it all and I had it all—but somehow it was hollow. I remember talking about love, but realized that I had never felt love. As I had done at St. Mary's, I gave instructions to women who wanted to learn about the Church. I even fell in love in a little priestly way: I caught myself combing my hair and shaving when one of them was coming over. I had a fantasy of romantic behavior. I probably over-romanticized love in many ways, like any inexperienced lover would. I had what I call "good bad thoughts" in those days. We priests used to hear about missionaries in the jungles of South America who had secret wives, secret lives. I fantasized a lot about becoming a missionary and finding perfect love in the jungle.

My confessions at the time were of these bad thoughts, but they were "healthy bad thoughts." I was lucky. I struggled for the want of love. I wanted people to like me, but I didn't let them. I reached out, but also kept up the wall. As for the priests I lived with and those directing my life from the chancery, I felt that someday they'd appreciate me and they'd realize how good I was and how much I meant to them. I was clearly in need of help—I'd become completely dependent on the approval of others.

Now, as I look back, I see my fault in this situation, because I kept any weakness well hidden. I had to be strong and tough. I never exposed my own needs for love or trust or risk. No priest did in those days. We were the Church and the Church was never weak or wrong or indecisive. Not sharing emotions, or denying their existence, sets up a collision course with the reality of those emotions—a collision course that I strongly believe endangers every priest, then *and* now. Dealing with emotions becomes a matter of luck and honesty. Priests—all human beings, really—must be able to confront the emotional challenges of being alone so often inside their world. It is in death that we face our emotional challenges.

I came to face a kind of death at Sacred Heart. This juncture, as horrible as it was, eventually led to my being knocked out of my isolation. But let me tell the story as it happened. Because of my youth work, I started holding dances in partnership with the Knights of Columbus. The dance hall, located downtown, became very popular throughout the city. We'd have maybe 300 or 400 kids each evening. We had our own band and orchestra, and held parties for Halloween, New Year's, spring, etc.

Bishop Grimmelsman hated the Knights of Columbus—just as he hated the Benedictines. I think that early on, the Chaplain of the Knights of Columbus, Monsignor Sprigler, had somehow antagonized the bishop, who forever after hated the Knights. Whenever we did anything with that group, Bishop Grimmelsman got upset—and we did a lot with them. Any time the bishop was against something, we all were for it, and vice-versa. This was a fascinating way to run a church, don't you think?

Finally, our group and our fun—our antics—created too much attention for the Knights, for Sacred Heart, and for a young priest. The bishop called me in to his office. "Stop It!" he said. I asked why. "Because I said so." I tried to explain that it was really one of the few activities available in town for teens. It was special for them and we weren't really doing anything wrong. There had been no trouble of any note. I managed to make it out of the meeting intact. I was getting brave in talking back to the bishop. But he got me back, as only a bishop can. We continued to attract huge and growing crowds from throughout the city. One Knights' youth dance even got featured in the local major newspaper. He shot me down for good once media publicity started. Along with so much else, he didn't like the media, either.

Chapter 6
Learning to Die and Rise Again

"I regret having ordained you a priest," the bishop said to me. It was 1957 and Bishop Grimmelsman was shouting at a 32-year-old priest—me. "I am sorry I did it. It was a mistake, and I am getting you away from me," he said. He sounded like the voice of one very angry God. "You're going out of Evansville. You are leaving here and you are never coming back. You will die there," he said. The meeting lasted only moments. He yelled. I tried to explain. He yelled all the more. It really hurt. I left that meeting the world's biggest failure. Yet I didn't have the strength to quit. In a few months things might be different; I tried to focus on that thought. I couldn't even bring myself to tell anyone what the bishop had said. The very man who had ordained me considered it a mistake. It was as if God had made the mistake. It was very painful.

In course of the tirade, I had learned that I was to be sent to St. Mary's Church, in Barr Township, near the rural area of Loogootee. In the seven years since my ordination, I had worked primarily in Evansville, the diocese's major hub. Loogootee was farm country, Father Aloysius country, about as far from Evansville as one could get and still be in the diocese. It was a death sentence. The voice of God sent me to stay at St. Mary's "until you die."

A few weeks later, I packed my few belongings and left the city for the country to the north. Two hours' drive that—at the time—was a journey back nearly 100 years. That county still had many people who spoke German. There was also a small enclave of Irish whose forebears had built the Wabash-Erie Canal and had worked on the railway. I moved to St. Mary's wishing more than a little that the bishop could defrock me for stupidity and end my humiliation, but even he could not do that. There in St. Mary's Church I hid as well as a pastor can hide, and as I hid I began to grow.

One of the first people I met was an old woman named Cecilia Brothers. Called "Celi," she was a small, bent over, sunken-eyed lady of 86. To me that was ancient. I took her Communion through the spring and learned that she was the last of seven sisters and one brother who had all lived on this farm without marrying. The family was known to be eccentric. Celi often wore three dresses on top of each other. She drank holy water out of the font. It took me a long time to figure out where the water was going. The farm was just as eccentric—a mess. There were eight private chicken coops, one for each sibling, falling over on one another. No animals of any sort remained. Overgrown fields surrounded the home. Celi had some sort of mental condition that often caused her to wander off. Once, when I organized a search party for her, we found her four miles away from home. There was no one to take care of her, so I brought her home with me until we could get her in a nursing home. She thought we were married. When I showed her the guest bedroom, she asked me which side of the bed I was going to sleep on. Celi died during the early summer at the nursing home. The previous pastor had arranged with her that she leave her farm to St. Mary's Parish. An ironic gift, assessed to be worth all of $150 per acre.

The farm was the challenge I needed. I threw myself with great energy into that 80-acre farm. I cleaned out fencerows. I gardened. I found help and help found me. The Amish community in the county was (and still is) sizeable. My Amish neighbors, the Graebers and Lenegachers, were a great help. My Catholic neighbors, the Matthews, Hopkins, Norris's, also volunteered to help me with the farm in a trade of labor. We worked side by side, I on their crops and they on St. Mary's. Leave no doubt who got the better end of that deal. I bloomed with the fields. We plowed and planted. We added cattle. And through the continuum of seasons, I healed myself over the course of 18 months. It was my first lesson in weakness and I began to grow strong.

Spending those 10 years at St. Mary's was one of the best lessons Bishop Grimmelsman could have forced upon me, although I doubt he intended it as a gift at the time: Bam! Down came his hand on the table—funny how I can still hear that chilling sound today. Life at St. Mary's-Barr Township was not as desolate or isolated as I had feared. I healed there, but even with my fond memories, I realize today that those times were not all perfection and joy.

I drank a lot during my time at St. Mary's, more so than before or after. Once, a group of priests from Daviess County went south to the best restaurant in Evansville, F's Steak House. We could not get seated right away, so we just kept drinking at the bar. I wound up getting sick all over the table.

Being a priest is a lonely life. For many priests, alcohol and the priesthood go hand in hand. I was a binge drinker at the time, going long stretches without alcohol, but unable to stop once I started.

Slowly other events began to fill my mind and the drinking binges stopped. Those events culminated in Vatican II. The changes made as a result of Vatican II came slowly, especially in the rural parishes. Still, at St. Mary's-Barr Township, I found myself part of an informal group of priests from the area. In addition to excursions to Evansville for dinner, we had lunch and golfed together— a support group before priests had support groups!

Being young priests, the changes that were coming naturally interested us. We invited some Jesuit priests from a nearby seminary to come over and teach us about Vatican II Christology, Morality, Ecumenism, and Theology. We received the inside scoop from the best teachers in the Church. The Jesuits know everything before anyone else. Vatican II presented seemingly limitless possibilities. We priests relished the changes. We didn't talk about them to the faithful, of course; we didn't want to "confuse" the poor layfolk. We were so full of ourselves.

Together with a good friend of mine, another young priest from a nearby parish, I got motivated to go down to Evansville and see the bishop. It was 1964. We went to him to ask permission to turn the altar around in these rural churches. We were tickled about the visit. We knew exactly how the meeting would go. Bishop Grimmelsman was nothing if not predictable. We went in and sat down. The bishop stood there looking out his window over downtown Evansville. He never looked at people when he spoke. He said, "I guess you want..." grumble, growl, grumble, growl, "... with the altar." "Yes, Bishop," we said. "I guess you think I should..." grumble, growl, growl, grumble, "... with the altar." "Yes, Bishop," we replied, waiting each time for the growling to subside. "I guess you think this..." grumble, grumble, growl, growl, "... is going to make everyone stay Catholic and be good." "Yes, Bishop." He looked at us and there was, for an instant, a faint glimpse of a smile. It was the only time I ever saw him smile.

So we turned the altars around. What did we risk going in there? And what did the bishop risk by giving his approval? Considering the risk is very important. Taking the risk is even more vital. Risk is tied to weakness. Risk puts you in a position of being seen as stupid, brazen, reckless—in short, weak. If you are weak, you admit you don't have all the information, or all the answers. You can learn and change if you are weak. Power becomes protective: Bishop Grimmelsman taught me that. Bishops must protect us from evil. Bishops must exert constant parental vigilance over their priests. Bishops must protect us from ourselves, even if that means keeping us from ourselves. Often bishops don't use their intuition, they just use their power. It's sad.

To a young priest in 1964, nothing was riskier or scarier than saying Mass in English, especially while facing the congregation. I remember feeling terrified in saying my first Masses that way—and I had gotten myself into the situation. I said the Mass looking intently and directly down at the book. I was so shy about it. But I grew out of it. And so my first macho, simple, oblivious, anxious life ended and I healed there in Barr Township.

I look back and see that in my first life, Jesus was a macho divine being—out of reach, not on the same plane as I. In those years I worked to reach that plane. In my youth, spirituality consisted of acts such as making my First Communion and observing all the rituals. I was very respectful and fearful of God. I made my confessions and kept First Fridays. If I did all of these individual observances, God guaranteed that I got into heaven. As a child and as a young priest, I was trying to earn a ticket to salvation. Doing these rituals and behaving appropriately as a favor to the Church was like getting my ticket punched. It sounds contrived today, but back then it was very respectful. It was what one did. More and more, I gave retreats and performed Forty Hours devotions to help people understand the purpose of living, yet I was having a hard time living myself. Slowly, I learned that the rules, the precision, the expectations all hurt. I saw Father John's story unfold. I stammered as friends turned on me. I felt the bishop's pounding on the table.

I was doing what I thought was the thing to do. I taught the "right," the correct way. So many times I missed the point. I was so caught up in the external ritual that I failed to look at what was inside. I saw God as just and fair and very macho. We priests and bishops represented that God, so what we did was God—wasn't it? Yes, the bishop's being sorry he'd ordained me was like God saying He was sorry He had made me—that was really a death for me—a death of the spirit.

At this time, I was giving catechism instruction to people and teaching them about the Church, but I was not feeding their souls. I taught them all the right things to do. But it was all...external. It was almost materialistic—we accumulated all these things and got to salvation. Before Vatican II, I was so caught up in ritual, meeting the outside goals and fulfilling roles, that I failed to think. God was simple, just and fair; He should be respected. That was it—or was it?

Part II

Chapter 7
My Secret Education

When I was somewhere around the age of 32, I died. The move to St. Mary's-Barr Township simply killed me. Failure terrified me. I was incapable of acting after my failure to please the bishop, only of reacting. The situation nearly paralyzed me. It made me realize that something important was missing, but I was lost as to what it was and—without any close companions or honest relationships—I had no one to turn to, to confide in, or to ask for help. Like many secular priests (priests unattached to a monastery or religious order), I was alone, adrift in the ocean.

After several years at St. Mary's, I sighted land, in a manner of speaking, along a highway of Chicago. It was around 1960. Following a vocations meeting, I was to return home via Chicago's O'Hare Airport. I drove my rental car past a cemetery. I had some time on my hands and, on impulse, I decided to stop there for a quiet moment. It held a significance for me: For the 10 years since ordination, I had lived my life, shared myself, blessed TV stations, converted lots of people, married couples, counseled the suffering, ministered to the poor and lame. I had done everything right. I was a success. Still, my bishop hated me.

I had done what I was told—well, most of what I was told. I became a priest. I hadn't spoken out harshly against the Church, even though I had sometimes wondered about Church authority. But all that time there had been an emptiness inside of me. Everything I had done was external, done to impress others. As I sat on a bench, staring at the tombstones, I thought, "If the world only knew my misery and isolation." I had never felt any support except for a handshake or a pat on the back. In fact, I had ceased to feel anything at all. I remember sitting in that cemetery thinking, "That's the way life is." I was ready to die.

I trudged back to the car and drove on toward the airport. In my somber mood, flipping the radio buttons, I happened to catch a radio show emcee pitching all the ways to get healthy and get ahead in life. His words caught my attention, "Make a list of all the things you really want, and you'll get them." I remember laughing to myself, saying, "That's crazy." I thought I had everything and look how miserable I was. Yet the thought stuck with me. When I got back to Loogootee, I sat down and made a list: Fix my eyes—I had been wearing prisms in my glasses, making it hard to read. The doctor had given me no hope, so I resolved to find another doctor; Follow a different ministry—maybe try being a counselor because I was not doing too well at teaching; Fall in love—I wanted an intimate relationship with someone; Consider leaving the priesthood—something I had never allowed myself to think about before.

Ironically, they all came true. I first went to the doctor and got contact lenses, a powerful solution to astigmatism, which allowed me to read more. Second, I talked to the people of St. John's High School in Loogootee about being a counselor, and they said yes, adding that it would be a neat thing for the high school. Eventually, I fell in love—but it took a lot longer than the glasses. For the first time, I honestly considered that my life in the priesthood was over; I had fulfilled all the things a priest did, so perhaps it was time to consider some other lifestyle. So, I went to St. John's and tried to become a counselor.

I assembled a lot of materials to help students think about where to go to college and was instrumental in getting a lot of them in—another personal success. I felt I was making a difference. But when I spoke with them about problems and difficulties, I found myself wanting to solve the problems for them. I realized I was trying to force my will on the students, and that they didn't want to do what I wanted them to. Soon I started to feel inadequate. I couldn't handle it. I knew this ministry was not working, and it made me feel even more inadequate. Instead of true counseling, I did vocational counseling—religious and collegiate.

It was a time of change, these months after the retreat in Chicago and during my work in high school counseling. Emotionally as weak as an infant, I waited—and listened to my desires for the first time. Suddenly, I knew I wanted to go back to school. Perhaps for the first time in my life, I wanted to learn what I needed to become a better listener for the students. Before my reflections in the cemetery and the chance encounter with a talk radio show, I thought I knew it all because *I was a priest*. But I was an empty priest. It began to dawn on me that my seminary education had only offered intellectual training—I never got any emotional training in my 12 years at St. Meinrad. None of us did. Because I entered the seminary at an early age, and my family's struggles with detachment and emotional distance, I was an empty vessel. Choosing to go to school would be a lesson in emotional training—more than I would ever have thought, even at that time.

I was terrified I'd fail. I didn't need to be publicly embarrassed again. Jim Lex, the one who saw seminary as an obstacle course, the one who spent all his time trying to outsmart the teachers, Jim wanted to go to school. I just could hear the snickers. To get going, I tested the waters at a friendly campus with a friend who was associate pastor at nearby St. Simon's Parish and who attended the University of Notre Dame during the week. He encouraged me to give it a try and share the drive with him. So it was through him that I accomplished my clandestine return to school. I got a B in Introduction to Counseling and a B in Counseling as Theory. It made me feel good—obviously I wasn't stupid.

Nevertheless, Notre Dame in the early 1960s was not a good experience for me. As a Catholic university, it attracted a lot of priests and nuns. The nightlife was quite active. They were all up there flirting and fooling around—all of them about as miserable as I was, but painfully unaware of it. All in all, a pathetic situation. After my ambivalent experience at Notre Dame came a stint at Loyola University in Chicago. It was expensive but a scholarship allowed me to attend the Institute of Counseling and Guidance for an entire summer.

From 1961 to 1963 I attended Notre Dame and Loyola. I commuted and it was damned inconvenient and expensive. Loyola was a great experience, but I couldn't keep it up. Commuting 500 miles round trip on a daily basis was completely incompatible with my parish responsibilities six hours to the south in Loogootee. At this point, no one in the chancery office knew I was even taking classes.

I was terrified that someone would hear of it and put a stop to it. I had no permission to be doing this. I knew I had to keep trying, so I quit Loyola and tried a third school. It was closer, cheaper, but an even bigger challenge. I thought I'd go there for a summer and take a course to see whether I could learn something helpful in the world of psychology.

So in 1964, without telling anyone, I enrolled at Indiana University—a huge, non-Catholic school just 50 miles away. I took a psychology course—Theories in Personality, I believe it was called. I had purposefully picked a difficult course—15 hours of prerequisites, none of which I had taken. Somehow, I convinced the administration to let me take the class. Although I attended class regularly, I didn't know the jargon. Deciphering the acronyms was like studying a foreign language. I regularly hid behind the other students so I would not have to answer questions. It was weeks before I knew the answer to one of the questions asked in class. What a relief! It turned out that I wasn't so dumb after all. I studied hard and at the end of the course received a "B." I was so proud. But I couldn't tell a soul, because no one knew I was taking the course. The university was heaven. That class opened my eyes to the purpose of education. For the first time I saw education as a way of enhancing myself.

Finally, I asked the bishop if I could take care of the parish while attending Indiana University, explaining that I had a chance for a scholarship. He laughed. "They won't give you a scholarship. Besides it won't do you any good anyway," he said. "But you'll probably go ahead and go anyhow—so go ahead." Coming from him, that was as close to a good luck wish as you could expect. I set out to find the scholarship.

I found out about the National Defense Education Act scholarships. These were Cold War scholarships to train high school counselors in helping teenage students reach their full potential, especially in the sciences, so we could keep up with the Russians. One year the NDEA scholarship funded around 30 students. I got the scholarship and the money.

With it, I earned my Master's Degree in counseling and guidance. Our NDEA group contained both men and women. At almost

40, I was the oldest among us. Before class, we would sit around and talk. I'd stop by a day-old bakery on the way to school, someone else would get coffee, and we soon had a regular little group going. We visited instructors, partied for holidays, and practiced what we discussed in class. From these people, I learned to be human.

We built a true community. For me, the first community that didn't revolve around sports. I was learning to share my inner self. It was a sharing I had never done with my family. This was the boy who entered St. Meinrad as a 98-pound, five-foot tall, spectacled squirt with an attitude. This was the seminarian who saw education as a labyrinth—where the teacher was the enemy. In mid-life, I was exploring my emotional "feminine" side. I was risking friendships. Life was different in Bloomington—or was I? Dr. Brown, the man who wrote the NDEA grant that funded our class, told me with his hand on my shoulder that I was the best student he ever had. It just knocked me over. These other students were great—yet he thought I was the best.

He was about five years younger than I and, at our first encounter, we immediately connected and he eventually became my doctoral advisor. We socialized on occasion, but it was very much a teacher-student relationship. I just couldn't get beyond calling him Doctor Brown. I admired him so much. As students, all of us served little apprenticeships of counseling other students while being taped. After reviewing my tapes, Dr. Brown would patiently inform me that I was being manipulative. I was leading the conversations and not-so-subtly telling students what was good for them. Each time he called me to task, I unsuccessfully tried to apply what he had said. It was so hard because I was hung up on learning all the "rules." What Dr. Brown showed me was that rules don't really run the world.

Eventually, I learned to listen to others' needs and to help them get those needs expressed. But each time I brought myself to a point where I wanted to share *my* needs, my friends were too busy telling me how they felt. It was difficult. Here I was, 40 years old and still an adolescent—especially in regard to my feelings and desires. I desperately wanted to connect with an individual. I even remember while driving back and forth from Loogootee to Bloomington seeing others driving alone and thinking how great it would be to connect our cars in a train so we could drive together.

My age aside, where I was truly unique at Indiana University was in being a priest—a priest with a parish. All the while that I attended classes, I still served at St. Mary's as parish priest. The parish community was wonderfully supportive of my adventure. We worked out a Mass schedule with only four days of Masses. I lived at the parish Friday through Monday, and stayed in Bloomington Tuesday, Wednesday, and Thursday nights. Each weekend, I'd come back and tell them what I learned.

During the week, to save money on campus, I roomed with a fellow also called Jim, a younger priest I had known casually for several years. He was from Evansville, too. He supervised the diocese schools and also studied school administration at the university. Jim offered me a support system; I saved him money. It was a match made in heaven. As I completed my Master's Degree in counseling, Jim pushed me to consider a doctorate. "They haven't kicked you out yet, have they," he asked. He kept on prodding me: "Why not go on?" "Are you afraid?" "Why not just keep going until they kick you out?" And so I did.

Chapter 8
Weakness Is My Strength

I was about to be reborn into a second life—my learning life; my mental life; my female life. In the first of my lives, I had learned the rules and the job, and how to be a lonely man. Now I was learning to be patient, gentle, and weak. In 1967, Bishop Grimmelsman finally retired and was succeeded by a Bishop Leibold. The change allowed Bishop Grimmelsman and me to re-form our relationship—to literally start anew.

After my brush with Bishop Grimmelsman in 1957 that got me "exiled" to the countryside, I had steered clear of him. Steering clear of him was not that hard to do, given my address. I had been ambivalent about him all along. I didn't like his priorities or performance as bishop, but I had never disliked him as a man. I have found that holding grudges takes too much energy. Looking back, I feel that I understood him far better than he understood me. I also realize that the bishop taught me to stand on my own two feet.

After he retired, I invited him up to St. Mary's-Barr Township to say the three-day prayer, Forty Hours. We had a surprisingly good time. He was complimentary about what I was doing with school and my studies. Now that he no longer felt responsible for me, no longer felt that he had to control me, he had turned out to be—or had turned into—a great guy. Power tends to get protective. Bishops want to protect everyone from evil. Bishops are like my grandmother: They are so afraid we are going to get proud that they feel the need to protect us from ourselves, even if it means keeping us from ourselves. They have to be the ultimate daddy for us all.

These kinds of revelations about power and authority came from re-examining my spirituality in these days of the 1960s. As a young man I believed in authority and respected authority. As "Father," I was an authority myself. I was faithful about saying Mass, reading the Divine Office, and going to confession.

With Vatican II, though, I began to see that the Catholic Church is the sum of many parts—most of them human. Her priests are human. Her bishops are human—and as humans, even bishops have doubts. It's a shame that priests and bishops are taught to know only the rules, because the Church is so lovely without all the rules. My new spirituality embraced that ideal and leaned more toward the dynamic that weakened the power of rules. At this time, I stopped the daily praying of the Divine Office. It was to be the first, but not the last, act of rebellion in my "marriage."

Near the end of my pursuit of a doctorate, I learned about a session on group dynamics offered in Niles, Illinois. I felt I had to go. Group counseling was something that had been missing from my studies. To affirm that I was getting the hang of the psychology classes and coffee house discussions I had enjoyed for the last two years, I needed to go. To feel ready for my dissertation and completion of my studies, I *had to* go.

National Laboratories, an East Coast psychology group, was the only organization in the country offering such conferences. Their staff traveled around the country giving these sessions near major cities. Mine was to be a 10-day intense group training session. It cost $600. I had to borrow the money from a friend at graduate school. At this time, my parish salary was $100 per month, plus I was earning $1,200 a year with my teaching assistantship. I also had tuition and books to pay for. But when I really wanted something, I didn't mind begging for it!

The workshops targeted practicing psychologists and psychiatrists, so National Laboratories would have to bend the rules to take me in. But again, in the special way I have of talking people into allowing me to do dangerous things, I talked them into it. Being a priest helped. I've never been sure why I felt so compelled to go. Maybe it was my ego—a desire to prove myself with these other practicing doctors. Maybe it had something to do with group dynamics being new and cutting edge, and the fact I knew nothing about it. I was afraid and excited. "This could change my life," I thought, driving up to the conference. "I might not even come back." It was a prophetic thought: the Jim Lex who went up there was not the Jim Lex who came home.

At that time, group dynamics was considered some sort of hocus-pocus, almost pagan. It was a dangerous, uncharted area I had just talked myself into. Also, it was a cold February and I looked forward to swimming in the resort's heated indoor pool between sessions. Maybe some wine and a few good meals—as compared to the fare we made ourselves in student housing back at the university. Yes, this was going to be good. The resort even had snowmobiles.

I was the lone novice among 27 psychiatrists and psychologists. Before the week finished, two of them had been hospitalized for stress—the session got out of hand quickly. National Laboratories promised "...small group activities and interactions for educational study with an opportunity for input and practice." It was learning through doing. All of these experiences were brand new in the 1960s. The leaders promised us life in a fishbowl, but at the five-day halfway point, it had already become a shark tank. The plan called for the group to be given a topic to dissect, discuss, and resolve as a group. The intent was to build trust. But suddenly—often cruelly—someone would assail that trust. A lot of latent anger and other negative feelings were unleashed, along with demonstrative sexuality. Living in the open atmosphere of the group, we all found power in saying anything we felt, or asking any question we wanted. I am sure it probably started out innocently enough. But it turned ugly. These professionals lost no time doing a trip on one another. Living in a group with no rules, it was so tempting. Working from the theory that no outsider can teach "group," that the facilitators should allow the group to "do group," we seduced the leaders. The group took charge. It was free booze, free drugs, free sex, and free self-destruction.

All of these strong, smart people resorted to booze and sex to cope with the unique challenges of the group. Often, they directed their challenges at me—the only priest in the group. They seemed to find my vocation amazing, disgusting, or otherwise intriguing, because they had caught me in their web. They demanded answers to such questions as: "Why are you a priest?" "Who do you...?" "What do you...?" "What are you hiding from?" "Who do you think you are?" "Why are you hiding behind that collar and the Church?" "Who ever asked you to help them?" "Who are you anyway?"

When I tried to explain my calling, every answer or attempted explanation brought on more questions. No one accepted my tale. They seemed threatened by everything about me and my life. They grilled me and then offered mistrust. They laughed at me. And yet they somehow admired me. Even so, they found me to be naïve—which of course I was.

This training session marked my final break with my first life. It brought out my feelings. I got angry, upset—I felt so many conflicting emotions that I couldn't even keep track of them. The group found ways to attack everything about me and my life. They taunted me—the naïve priest who was still in school. I began to think, "Hey, I am far from home. I can do anything I want to here and no one will know..." All of us staying together in the same place was difficult—not in the least because a lot of the women gave me keys to their rooms. At one point during the challenges to me and my priesthood, I must have looked particularly pathetic because a man in the group confronted me. At first I thought he was going to hit me, but then he kissed me square on the lips. At that point I just about lost it. His being gay affected me.

What had I done to encourage that? What signals had I sent? Was I gay? After this he kept staring at me during meals. Smiling. Winking. It was almost like being stalked—or at least that's what it felt like to me in my worn-out state. The 50 questions game we kept playing within the group forced me to deal with that kiss. I had to talk about it. I had to deal with it within the group. Such talk was definitely a new experience. Unintentionally, the others in the group rescued me. They helped me realize that I could not take responsibility for everything. With that insight, I put a large piece of my past behind me. I gave up guilt and I gave up control. I could have given up entirely and left the group while in crisis, but I chose not to. A turning point.

I gave in to the weakness. I embraced it. My answer to every question became, "I don't know." And suddenly, almost magically, I became the powerful one in the group. I was not afraid to say, "Hell, I don't know why, or what, or who I am." Because I was able to give up and let go, there was strength. By doing that, I became smart. Boom! Just like that, it had happened. I realized these people around me, below me, and in my face weren't smart, they were just pushy as hell. I saw their self-centeredness. They were just lonely bastards looking for something more and that's why they challenged me—to see if there was something more. Given the anonymous freedom to abandon my vows, I could have slept with the women. I could have left the priesthood. People in the group had offered me jobs. I had a chance to take the money and run. I chose not to do so. Those four short words are extremely important to me: "I *chose* not to." Before this time, I had never really felt that I'd had any choice.

Whether it was choosing not to quit or choosing not to stay, those were strong words. I had the freedom of free love, and I chose not to. I had the freedom of denial and I chose not to. I had the freedom to condemn and I chose not to. I had the freedom to attack and I chose not to. Because I had nothing to prove—other than my complete ignorance and my well-known stupidity and naïveté—I became smart. My weakness became my strength at that hour, on that day. My whole perspective on weakness just came to me in that instant. Suddenly everything had changed. I have spent the rest of my life applying what I learned about being "weak" from a bunch of sharks in Niles. Before, I'd never even felt adequate. I'd never had a good opinion of myself. Now suddenly I was a fine person. I could see the good—and the evil—in me. I left Niles thankful to be alive and not in a mental hospital. But I also left having chosen to remain a priest and having become a lot smarter than I was when I first strolled in looking for the pool and some wine.

When I came back to Bloomington, Nancy Weaver, whose husband had lent me the money to go, noticed a change in me. She noticed I was not afraid anymore. She and I discussed the manipulative things I had done before. Nancy explained that before the Niles trip, she had been afraid of me. She didn't trust me. And for good reason. Nancy was an attractive woman, cute in a safe, Doris Day kind of way. I was probably harboring a secret admiration for her that she intuitively felt. She was always guarded around me, but when I came back from the battles of Niles, she found a new Jim Lex—a man she could readily trust. The romantic idealist had disappeared and a realist had taken his place.

These talks with Nancy made me consider what the differences were—how I could have been so transformed in less than two weeks. Experiencing this transformation meant that I had to confront my sexuality fully. Before Niles, my sexuality was hidden and only emerged as sinful fantasies in direct contradiction to my vows. After Niles, I accepted my sexuality and immediately began to grow both mentally and spiritually. I had gone to the wall but I had not fallen apart. Hello and goodbye to the ghost of Bishop Grimmelsman. I kept my composure and admitted I didn't know anything. This time, however, I didn't get sent to Loogootee for it. I got my Doctorate in Educational Psychology instead.

Dr. Brown told me later that I had gotten one of the highest scores ever on the written part of the doctoral test. I think the reason was that I was comfortable. I could express myself more clearly. I knew what was going on—for the first time in my academic life. I was 42 years old. At the time I was finishing up, my roommate, Jim, was ready to move on, too. He had a chance to leave the Diocese of Evansville and work for the National Catholic Education Association in New Jersey. In order to do that, however, he was required to find someone to fill his position as Superintendent of Catholic Schools.

Each week, we'd sit and try to come up with someone to take the job. We'd ask the priest and he'd say something to the effect of "Hell, no." Or Bishop Leibold would turn him down. And we'd keep looking. Finally, after about the fifth refusal, Jim and I decided that I could do the job. Jim went and asked the bishop. About a week later, the bishop sent me a letter expounding on the providence of God and His ordination that I should accept this position because of Jim's leaving at the time when my studies ended. "It is a blessing that you take this job," the bishop wrote.

I knew God's providence had little to do with it. I was the sixth choice. Because it looked dangerous, I said yes. It was a done deal from the start. After ten years, I left St. Mary's-Barr Township and the town of Loogootee. It was to be the only assignment I ever had for more than a few years at a stretch. I went there to die, and was reborn; I lived. The entire journey that had originally seemed like a banishment had turned out to be an excellent experience instead.

Chapter 9
My Jealous Marriage

Stepping back a few months, to the time before Niles when I was still a student at Indiana University, I can see how completely I rationalized my celibacy. If I could go out and have a date and dinner with someone, the woman's needs and mine would be filled at the same time. That seemed pretty good, so I went out more and more with different women. Bloomington gave me comfortable anonymity. Getting married wasn't really my goal, but I wanted that kind of closeness and I wanted friends. Even if I didn't want marriage, I wanted platonic intimacy and trust-filled relationships. I kept looking to different women and found a little intimacy here, a little intimacy there. At the same time, I had no hope of ever finding any one person to fill my needs. Until....

It all started because of a sprained ankle. While finishing a teaching assistantship at the university in 1967, I enjoyed some fairly unlimited personal freedom. I had left the parish in anticipation of the new job in Evansville. I took a spring break vacation. Several of the graduate students, both men and women, decided to go to Phoenix for a week. It was great fun. Unfortunately, while horsing around by the pool, I sprained my ankle. So, when I returned to finish the semester as a teacher, I was on crutches. A bright and kind woman in one of my classes slipped me a medicine bottle after class with a lipstick kiss inside on a piece of paper. The instructions on the outside of the bottle said, "Apply to where it hurts. Love, Maggie."

She would have given the same note to anyone—to a woman teacher or to a teacher who was 109 years old. The gesture meant nothing to her other than an acknowledgment of how hard it was to teach and lug books around the campus while on crutches. I, on the other hand, was deeply touched that anyone cared. Suddenly, I was in love. Enter Maggie, a vivacious, beautiful 28-year-old, devout Presbyterian with a critical eye, a witty tongue, a big heart, and a love for conversation, music, and fine dining. She became my lifeline for the next several years. I was a 42-year-old priest with a cynical eye, a laughing manner, a needy heart, and a love for conversation, music, and fine dining.

A few days later I invited her to dinner and she said yes. No big deal. She was still just being nice. One thing led to another—picnics, Frisbee, bowling, cards, music. We both were looking for companionship and intimacy. Neither she nor I was interested in permanence at the start. I still had other close women friends with whom I dined or took in movies. Some were her friends, too. Initially it wasn't any big deal. Gradually I began to find my time with Maggie more fulfilling. It was trust-filled and wonderful. How naïve I was! I was a priest. Alone, craving closeness.

All priests confront this issue. They try to tell themselves, "I don't have to take responsibility. I don't need to take the initiative. Women flirt with me and I just receive it." Some priests never get past that point. What is this, this celibacy? What *is* celibacy? What does it mean? In the 1960s I was a tease, but I was a celibate tease. I was not married, not physically intimate, not emotionally intimate. Unattached to women, I was married to the Church. I kept looking for intimacy and didn't really know what celibacy was. I had rationalized that celibacy meant being in love with many and not just one. Kind of a moderate celibacy.

It sounded good, but it was not too smart. I had a jealous partner in the Catholic Church. She would hold for none of this running around. My moderate view of my life commitment caused confusion for these women friends of mine. They would hear that they were special to me—and they felt individually that I was special to each one of them. Because they didn't have these other men or people around from whom to get sustenance and nurturing, they were hurt and offended that I wouldn't commit. With Maggie, my moderate celibacy theory unraveled. As a Presbyterian involved with a Catholic priest, Maggie was really confused. She thought I was putting her on. I wanted to be a priest, but so much wanted the closeness.

Maggie's mother helped in her own little way by sending Maggie newspaper clippings about priests quitting the priesthood and the horrible things that happened to them. She worked hard to convince Maggie that if she loved me, she'd let me go. Nevertheless, during spring break the following year, I went with Maggie to visit her parents. They didn't know how to take me or to treat me. They didn't know what the hell I was after. She was their little girl. I was an old man. It was tough. I admit, I wanted it all: the priesthood and love. I wasn't going to leave, but I was in love. I fantasized that we could be just friends and go off and do missionary work together. She was a religious person and a very good person, too. I wanted to somehow arrange to "have her around"—intimately but platonically—and still be a priest, still be uncompromised. She had all the qualities of a perfect partner.

So we kept seeing each other and building this wonderfully deep but totally platonic relationship. While I was debating what to do, my mother and my sisters came up. They feared I would leave the priesthood, but they tried to be nice and were actually very supportive. It was a difficult, yet exciting, creative, evolving, life-giving time. Dr. Brown even offered some help—just to put it on the table as an option without any pressure. He, as a Lutheran, saw a place for me within the Lutheran Church. There I could minister and be married to Maggie. Another option he offered was to hire me as a teacher at the university.

A mutual male friend often listened to my agony. I didn't want to leave the priesthood. I told him I felt that I was supposed to be a priest—that was what God wanted me to do. I was gradually working toward a decision, but I must have been going very slowly. In the end, he made my decision for me. In going over to comfort Maggie, he "stole" her. She married him instead of me. It was the saddest day of my life. They later divorced after 15 years of marriage. Meeting and knowing Maggie was the peak of my life. Our unique relationship lasted two years. My life with Maggie led me to understand that someone could choose to love me—someone who was not a relative by birth. I'd never even kissed her.

Perhaps my other needs were met at the time—enough so that I could handle the relationship without panic or too much testosterone. By the time I met Maggie, in 1967, I wasn't drowning, just adrift. Ten years earlier, it might have been a different story—or at least had a different ending. Also, my inner age probably had something to do with the platonic relationship. Even though I was

42, I had never been in love. I had felt infatuation, but nothing like my feelings for Maggie. I certainly didn't want to screw it up with sex. I was an adolescent hanging out with the prettiest and wittiest woman in the neighborhood. She respected the Church enough not to encourage me to be physical. This respect, and her love of life, were what was so strong about my attraction to her. I suppose it is hard to understand that we could be so completely devoted and not be physical. Had I crossed that line with her...well, there would have been no return.

Even though she has happily remarried, I still love Maggie and occasionally visit her. I never really got over this "love affair." I never wanted to. I have gone out with others and been intimate with others, but it's never been the same. I am weak in this respect. My love for and with Maggie shows the truth of the paradox of weakness giving you strength. Loving someone like that fills a person up. It is power-giving when you need each other equally.

Was ours really a marrying kind of love? I will never know. Having seen my friends who quit to marry and who are now seemingly fulfilled and happy, I often wonder if deep inside they carry a resentment because of what they had to give up. If I had quit, would I have regretted it? This struggle may be easier to understand in terms of the Church. For example, the homily is the riskiest place during Mass. I am terrified of preaching. But I don't stop doing it. I risk it each Sunday because I need the people. A priest can't preach to an empty church. The people in turn, need me, a priest, to offer Mass and a sermon. I need them and they need me, and I get strength from them and they get strength, I hope, from me. And so we go forward.

Relationships. Church relationships are supportive and risky. Intimate relationships are supportive and risky. It is the same. My so-called friend took Maggie away and I ate it. I didn't know a soul who could listen to my pain. In those days, priests had no support groups or confidants. Today, I have a few priest friends with whom I could share my pain. At that time, I just kept myself busy and thought I was handling the loss fairly well—until one day I went to get a haircut.

Somehow, the loss kicked in that day and there was Jan. Jan was a gorgeous, sexy beautician who cut my hair. I had a reaction. It was my dirty little trick. Jan and I began what was a brief, passionate affair. We shared a cottage in Hawaii. We shared rooms in hotels. I was venting my anger at Maggie. Jan, this loving, generous woman wanted to get married. But that wasn't my fantasy, not this time. When I finally broke it off, Jan smacked me good across the face. She cussed me out and threatened me. I deserved every word. Jan was the one woman I feared for years. But she was a better person than my fears made her out to be. Recently, I ventured to look her up and we talked. She is still generous and kind. She even offered to let me move in with her and her adult children if I ever needed a place. Jan got me over Maggie. And I got on with my work.

I renewed my commitment to the priesthood at this point, one little bit at a time. The point was that I was able to make the commitment even if only in the short term. I have made it hundreds of times in my life since. Looking back, I can see that even though I could never commit to another person—not even to Maggie—I seem to have a very deep-seated commitment to the Church. The commitment isn't to the institution, but to the people—the Body of Christ. In seminary, I came to fully embrace the concept that humans are part of the whole that is Christ. This understanding is a catholic understanding. I am fully committed to the unique sacrifice offered to God with each Mass. This, too, is a catholic commitment. But is it a commitment or a habit? Is it fear or a choice? Could I find it outside of the Roman Catholic priesthood? I doubt it.

I have successfully evaded the decision to leave for my entire life. I wonder now how much risk I was ever willing to take. It's not just my risk. Quitting the active priesthood risks all whose lives I have ever touched. The people whom I have touched with the sacraments are all part of the Body of Christ—the hands, the eyes, the mouth of Christ. To them I feel a great debt. Leaving the priesthood would mean that, in a sense, I had left them—left the Body. To many people, a priest represents the fullness of the Catholic

Church. For them, we are as far as they get in study and experience. My remaining a priest bows a bit to them: to my desire to keep them in the family, so to speak. Any priest knows many people who will tell him that he is the only reason they remain a practicing Catholic.

It's vanity to a small extent; it's holding on to my reputation. Reputation is a hell of a thing. I was in a workshop once where participants had to write down the ten most valuable things to them and give them away to the group: honesty, my car, my health... When I did it, the last thing I was willing to give up was my reputation. I am a pleaser still. The difference is that now, as opposed to when I was 15, 25, or 35, I am more selective about those I try to please.

Nevertheless, having a good reputation may be as much as 50 percent of the reason I kept my position in the Church. Despite that, I stayed. I grew emotionally and my spirit soared.

Chapter 10
Going to School as the Boss

I worked as superintendent of the diocese schools for five years. I had no educational background, but my degree in psychology was valuable because not many people had the training at that time. I was trendy. Besides, with Vatican II still the bee in everyone's bonnet, the diocese didn't need an educator in the job; the entire system needed a psychologist.

From 1967 on, the entire Church was in a critical period of transition. It was on the local level that the Vatican II changes really took place. That era witnessed an unsettling of the rock the Church was founded on. It was also the era of the Vietnam War and the Civil Rights Movement. Everyone in the United States in 1967 was busy criticizing anyone in power. The public mocked or openly defied authority. Within this context, it wasn't surprising that Catholic schools faced turmoil. Suddenly, people weren't automatically sending their children to Catholic schools. Suddenly the priests and sisters were leaving and the teachers felt alone. Layfolk did not know how to teach religion. Parishes were divided over whether or not to begin offering religious education for children not attending Catholic schools. It had never been an issue before. Fights. Emotions. Fear. It was an exciting time—I was thrilled to be there.

The turmoil also caused me my share of stress. Although my memories of the job are nearly all good, I just about killed a priest during those early months in the job. I must have been tense on some level. The "near-murder" crisis was due to the annual budget of the school office. I had followed the guidelines set out for me by an administrative priest in the treasury office to the letter. I knew him. I trusted his advice. I went into the committee expecting easy approval. The committee had serious questions about my methods, and there sat my old buddy agreeing with the committee. He didn't support me and basically made fun of me for presenting the budget the way he had told me to present it.

After the meeting, when I saw him in the parking lot walking to his car, I went up to him, grabbed him by the neck and screamed at him, "If you ever do that to me again I will kick the shit out of you!" I remember the words exactly. He was several inches taller than me and weighed nearly 240 pounds. He could have squashed me, I am sure, but he seemed very shaken. I know I surprised him. As I left, I immediately calmed down. By the time I was driving out of the parking lot I was laughing to myself, picturing the encounter, and laying odds that I could not have done it—beaten him up—if I had tried. He was too big. I have never been that mad in my life—before or since. That was 100 percent rage. Most of the time, though, I loved the job. I also loved the other outlets that allowed me to minister, and I loved the parishioners I came in contact with as associate pastor. While working in the school office I served concurrently as associate pastor to an assortment of Evansville parishes. With the exception of St. John's downtown, all were country parishes surrounding Evansville. Moving that much provides the chance to meet lots of people, but you really have to work fast at building nurturing relationships.

My dissertation still needed to be finished. Over the next several years, I squeezed that into the equation as well. I wanted to write my dissertation on weakness and strength. But Dr. Brown said I had to choose a broader theme. I picked group dynamics. I went to St. Meinrad and offered students there a course on group dynamics. They could discuss anything they wanted—no structure. Then I compared their honesty, openness, and trust at semester's end with that of a control group who did not take the course. Actually, there wasn't a lot of difference. Still, it got me my doctorate in 1972. My work on the subject of "weakness" was my real love, my baby, my child for this world. Also in 1972, I reared this child to maturity with a self-published book, *My Weakness is My Strength*. The book was a little paperback text about how you have to be weak to be vulnerable, be vulnerable to be loved, and how you have to show weakness to both receive love and be able to give it in return. Weakness is the key to love and strong relationships.

By 1968, I was living at St. John's Church-Evansville with Father Pat. Next-door were some Sisters of St. Benedict—some of them became my closest lifelong friends. We had great times. I was still seeing Maggie during this period. She was my one-on-one. But St. John's was also a platonically intimate and loving place. Father Pat and I showed the nuns how to drive a car. They invited us over to see their new clothes when the old habits went and new modern habits were allowed. Pat and I had grown up together at St. Joseph's Parish in Evansville. He is a bit younger than I, but his older brother had been in my class at St. Joseph's School. The nuns supported our ministry and we supported theirs. St. John's Church was in the central city area of Evansville. It was a middle-to-low income area at that time, rapidly declining as wealthy African American families began to integrate and move out of the area. The parish was in transition.

We two priests needed to stir things up a bit. Pat and I started a Midnight Mass on Saturdays to drum up business. At that time, the Saturday evening Mass had not been approved, but people out late on Saturday really wanted to get that Mass in before going to bed. We figured it would be popular and bring people in from the out-side—with money for collections! We had dueling homilies during that late Mass. One of us would start to preach and the other—sitting in the pews—would interrupt. We'd have a big argument about interpretation and viewpoint. It was very popular. We'd fill the church. People really got into it. They'd start affirming or boo-ing. Of course, there aren't too many priest pairs who could do this stunt. Pat and I were a great team—no ego collisions between us to mar this experiment. The egos of some other priests got in the way, though. There were inevitable complaints about the nuts down-town. Soon we had the chancellor peeking through a crack in the door from the back of church. He spied on us, but we were OK and it worked well.

I became involved in what was finally some positive politics within the diocese. We had Bishop Leibold, who gave me more of a mandate. He was a great bishop, very much into the changes of Vatican II. He wanted to set up a personnel board and I became involved with the Priest Placement Committee for the diocese. There were four of us, each representing a different age group. It was a telling experience. Without a lot of fanfare we'd try to visit priests to negotiate assignments quietly. At every visit, somehow, they knew we were coming. Priests are the biggest gossips in the world. There isn't perhaps any more closed, more mistrustful a group of men in the world than priests.

We called ourselves the Night Riders—because that's how we were viewed. We had to come in at night for visits—after we had finished the day's work of our parish or chancery jobs. The idea was to make visits and get the priests' input about assignments. Where did they want to go? What did they want to do? The men couldn't say. Maybe they weren't used to being asked. Maybe they were just going to be miserable no matter what. At least with the old way, they could blame the bishop. No one was ever completely candid. They couldn't share their deep feelings. I guess none of us wanted to make our own decisions at that time. The priests on the council finally got scared. The Priests' Council voted us out—voted to dissolve the personnel board. So Bishop Leibold made us diocesan consultors—in this manner, he beat the vote and went around the rules. Bishops like to be in charge, even progressive ones! It all worked out eventually. Today the personnel committee still functions—functions well even. But it took us a long time to get everyone on board to accept just the basic idea.

Creating a diocesan council was another trauma that resulted from the Vatican II changes. When setting up the first council, the diocese had a faction that definitely wanted a priest as the president of the diocesan council. There was another faction that demanded equally loudly that it be a layperson. One of the priests who supported a layperson in this new role came to me and asked me to be the priest nominee. I was considered far too dangerous, being fresh out of the university and a psychologist. I was sure to lose. I did. The poor priests were terrified of me, so they elected a wonderful, but quite radical layperson to the post. He did a great job. One of the nice things about my life at this stage was that I could do that—run to lose with grace. The lessons of weakness taught me that I didn't need to win.

The position of school superintendent allowed me to use my intuition and make some great moves for the diocese. One of them was to hire a Dominican sister who was in Evansville looking for work. On a 12-month leave from her convent, Sister Ann had private disagreements with her order and with where her life was going. She knew Father Pat through a former student of hers. Pat, Ann, and I met one evening over coffee. I immediately connected with her in a deep way. That evening, I made her Director of Religious Education for the diocese. I took an hour to make the decision—and hired her on the spot. It was one of the smartest decisions I ever made. She worked with me in the education office for a year while living upstairs in the second-floor apartment. I think a priest had hurt her. I never asked, and I still don't know for sure, but it was just a feeling I got from hints and what was left unsaid. I knew with Ann immediately that there were lines I couldn't cross.

Ann worked well with Sister Mary Charlotte, my proverbial right hand. We became a team. Mary Charlotte worked in the Catholic schools and Ann worked in developing the various parish religious education programs. She knew all the curricula, programs, and books of which I had no knowledge. Ann's rich background in religious education supported the fledgling programs and gave training to volunteer catechists. Outside of work, Ann was also an effective communicator. She was positive. Over the years, we have been good for each other—we have always called one another to spiritual exploration. Ann was and is always on the cutting edge of the Spirit. That is a good type of person to run with.

First, she was a woman who needed a break, a chance to soar. Second, she was a sister—my sister, someone who understood me. Third, she trusted me at a time when she did not trust, or even particularly like, men. She knew Pat trusted me so she took a chance with me. For that I am grateful. With Ann I found something close to the feelings I enjoyed with Maggie. Something clicked deep inside—something spiritual, wonderful and healthy. Ann, older than I, is a wise and stable woman. She helped me at the time we worked together because she knew what she was doing and had made her vows to this Church just like I had. Ann understood the Catholic side of it all—the mysterious pull.

With Ann, as with Maggie, my emotions were deep, intimate. Intimate—not sexual. It was not physical, but it was more than friendship. They touched something deep in my loneliness. They touched my sharing and my trust. I felt comfortable with them in a special, spiritual way. This closeness is crucial to good mental health, but priests don't find it often. These two women (careerwise, Ann in particular) mentored me in a fashion. Before them, my only mentor had been Father Paschal during those few years within seminary. It was healthy for me to be able to express my needs to them. They allowed me to nurse myself and, when I was with them, I could stop ministering to others' needs.

Chapter 11
Learning to be a Priest

As I grew into my second life, the past, my transforming experiences, and my friends all seemed to glide away. Other adventures took their place, and I was thrilled to be able to put this newfound emotion to good use. During the 1970s, I met and began working with a Trappist, Father Vincent Dwyer. An interesting educator and spiritual director, he fascinated me. A former navy man, he was from a monastery in Massachusetts. Father Vincent had attended Catholic University in Washington D.C. with Father Kenny, a priest from Evansville. He and Father Kenny got to be good friends because they shared similar philosophies about how people learn, and holistic approaches to education and spiritual direction.

At Father Kenny's behest, Father Vincent came to Evansville in 1972 to lead a priests' retreat. With dozens of others, I attended this retreat—one that affirmed what I felt to be true. Bringing Father Vincent to southern Indiana proved to be a big boost for the morale of local priests. It really brought about long-term changes in the attitudes and approaches to maintaining mental health among priests. Through the inner discovery process Father Vincent asked, "What are three things you would like to do? What are three things you are embarrassed about?" No one had ever asked priests these questions before, not to mention that Father Vincent expected an honest response. The experience with Father Vincent led us to form support groups for priests within the diocese. We learned to build trust and form bonds of friendship.

Father Vincent pioneered studies about meeting priests' needs and keeping priests stable. The intent was to enhance a priest's spirituality by treating him as a whole person. This was a new theology for the Church. Father Vincent challenged us to look inward, to what was going on in our heads and to affirm ourselves as complete humans. His approach involved not only group discussion and introspection, but also completion of psychological tests and exercises. For example, one section of the test included questions that probed how much time priests spent in the present moment. A self-actualizing person was eight times in the present to one in distraction. At the time, priests overwhelmingly scored four times in the present to one in distraction—including me. This "future-or-past" worry pattern led priests to become more tired and depressed. The pattern indicated that priests often felt God didn't hear their prayers.

Taking the test opened my eyes to the plight of my brother priests and to dangers of chronic worry. I began to write my thoughts in a journal and consciously noticed my distractions from the present. I taught myself to stay in the present for the day, or the morning, or for at least an hour. I found I was happier, healthier, more energetic. I began to note my worry-distractions in a journal over days and weeks: What's going to happen to me? Am I really going to leave and get married? Am I ever going to amount to anything? If I couldn't deal with it on that particular day, I wrote the thought down and forgot it. I didn't have to be distracted by the thoughts. If they were in the journal, I gave myself permission to relax. I focused only on what I could do that day. When a person is out there in the "future-or-past," he or she is out there alone. God is not in the past or the future. God is the always. God is the "I Am." God is now.

I still write down my distracting thoughts when they become overpowering. To this day several priest support groups, born of this time with Father Vincent, are still helping priests find their way. I was in a support group for 15 years. I drew from it confidence in expressing myself and my feelings. I found that many priests shared my feelings. That which is the most private is also the most universal. It was such a relief. I had been emotionally intimate with Maggie and Ann, and now we priests were learning to share, to be weak, and to be emotionally intimate.

Thank God for Father Vincent coming to the Diocese of Evansville. My experience went beyond participating. I was lucky enough to be able to assist Father Kenny and Father Vincent in their work with the Center for Human Development beyond Evansville. Around 1975, I began to help Father Kenny and Father Vincent give retreats. It grew into a passion that filled several years of my spare time. The strategy was that Father Vincent or Father Kenny would lead a retreat group through the process and I helped individual priests evaluate his psychological tests: the Personality Orientation Inventory, the Tennessee Self-Concept, and the Ministry Inventory.

After experimenting with priests, Father Vincent wrote multimedia programs for use with laypersons: Genesis 2 and Romans 8. Father Vincent hoped that priests who had been through the program would take these courses back to their parishes and use them. The concept was tremendously successful. Suddenly, we three were going everywhere—north, south, east, west, even to Korea and Europe—to lead these retreats. Ministers of all faiths seemed starved for what affirmation and understanding Father Vincent offered. I gave six of Father Vincent's retreats to Methodist ministers in New Jersey, actually to the entire Methodist governing body for the southern half of the state. They picked me to come rather than Father Vincent. I was so proud. Working with Father Vincent, I tested more than 3,000 priests. He tested another 3,000.

By 1984, Father Kenny was called back to work exclusively for the Evansville Diocese. Father Vincent began to be ill with problems that haunt him to this day— At the time of this writing, he is suffering from bladder cancer. In England and Australia, the programs are still running fairly strongly, but they have subsided in the United States. Unfortunately, the results of the personality inventories have never been published. Father Vincent holds a remarkable amount of information—it seems a shame we've never heard his whole story. Still, it's hard to hold onto the Trappist mentality while being such a world-renowned public figure. Maybe that, and not the illness, was why he just stopped.

I found the 3,000 priests I inventoried to be really good men— overwhelmingly so. They wanted to be hard workers and to serve the people. As a group, however, we also overwhelmingly blamed the seminary for all our problems. And we were—are—preoccupied with the past. Priests often think, "I am the only priest who has felt this way or had this trouble." A priest's entire training is to privacy. He is trained to keep secrets—confessions, fears, opinions. He is expected to live alone. Then, in the support groups stemming from Father Vincent's leadership, priests suddenly found that

71

they were not alone but that they shared the same pain and fear that comes from isolation.

Father Vincent's lesson was that as a whole, priests—indeed all ministers—have more feelings in common than one would expect, and that priests/ministers are more mentally normal than they think they are. Clergy are all equal—equally weak. Through the support groups stemming from these sessions, ministers and priests throughout the world learned, at least a little, to depend and lean on one another. Even though it involved testing and statistics, my work with Father Vincent was spiritual. The Holy Spirit was present in these small groups. God was there, "Where two or three gather..." (Mt 18:20) It gave me an appreciation of other priests' struggles. Our need for each other came out. None of us have "got it together." Even the leaders—the bishops and abbots—have the same temptations, frustrations, and problems.

My idea of God grew more ecumenical in my travels and work with Father Vincent. I remember being caught up in prayers, spontaneous praying, the respect for others and their feelings. How did God work through them? As my spirituality became less formal, it was more spontaneous. It was friendly and open. I saw that God needs us to bring His love into the world.

During this time—the 1970s and into the early 1980s—many, many priests traded active ministry for marriage, or left for reasons of personal frustration and loneliness. Many saw leaving as a sign of weakness, but I took their leaving as sign of their strength. These men were able to admit that they were weak and needed companionship or more tangible rewards. They had the courage to act. Many priests stayed and hid their fears in less acceptable ways.

When a priest decided to leave, or while he was deciding, he'd often come to talk to me. I believe that I counseled on some level—maybe over a cup of coffee, or at a ball game, or more formally—every priest in the diocese who quit in those times. What I offered each was a pat on the back, "You did a great job. And it is neat that God is now calling you to something else." I affirmed them, their work and their inner voices. From the parish, the hierarchy, the alma mater, and even, sadly, from their parents, brothers and sisters, they heard guilt, guilt, guilt. I offered them compliments.

James and William Lex
1927

Robert and James Lex
1938

Mother Marie, Mary, James, and Dorothy Lex
at St. Meinrad

73

*James Lex in
his "first life"*

1946

1950
ordination photo

1960

The island priest

James Lex, Santa

James Lex, cook

Compliments are easier to give and easier to hear when one stays in the present moment.

At the same time I worked with Father Vincent, I was making career moves. Running the administrative office of the Catholic Church in the post–Vatican II was not the place for a needy person. I wasn't getting many, if any, compliments at that time. But that was OK; Father Vincent and my close relationships gave me an outlet. However, my full time job in the school office provided many distracting thoughts. I spent a lot of time giving talks to smooth over the rapid changes of Vatican II. There were many school closings, and philosophy and staffing changes. Religious education began to be stressed—separate from the schools.

We had traditional and well-respected Catholic schools. To that we added a thorough religious education curriculum for public school students. People couldn't accept both ends. They were stuck with the thought that you couldn't have a good school and a good religious education program: they would be competitive. The idea caused a lot of fights, anger, and misunderstandings. The emotion of the exchanges excited me. Dealing with emotions was my thing— my main interest—at that time. In a way, the job was secondary.

I was very much in the public eye. This area of Indiana is 25 percent Roman Catholic, so Catholic news makes the news. At times I had a difficult job.

During my tenure, I helped develop a philosophy and mission statement for the schools. We developed a five-year plan for starting religious education centers in a number of spots around the diocese. We set up local school boards for schools to distribute the power to the laity and parents, we set up a foundation to finance students who couldn't pay, and we encouraged consolidation of schools to make them more viable. The need to work together from now on was the major new philosophy I brought to the schools. It wasn't just the priests and nuns. The parents had a role in the schools' success. And by upgrading the schools, we got a good base of some great teachers. I like to think I ushered in change in a positive way and kept the lid on some explosive situations.

People forget how scary and new the 1960s and 1970s were for the Church. Religious education training for the laity and giving parents responsibility in passing on the faith were strange for many people. A superintendent in a time of turmoil has to face it all. One time, all the priests turned against me because a teaching sister had (mis)quoted me as having said that we didn't need sisters. Obviously, a misunderstanding. Bishop Leibold called a meeting for all priests to discuss what had actually been said, and together we cleared it up. It taught me, though, how quickly everyone can turn on you. I learned to live with that uncertainty.

I think that a lot of priests, even old friends, saw me as the messenger of bad news and changes. I got blamed for the lack of teachers, for money problems, for everything. It helped that I was working as superintendent by choice. I chose to be superintendent, and I chose when to leave. As long Bishop Leibold was there, the job was fine. He liked my style and the way I treated the teachers and others. He supported my work to get a retirement fund for teachers, for example. But then he left after being appointed Archbishop of Cincinnati. The new bishop, Bishop Shea, came to Evansville in 1970. It took awhile to get acquainted, but it soon became obvious that he didn't like my style.

He often said in later years that the first time I met him, I had told him that the Latin School was a mess, was falling apart, and that it had to be closed. That is probably exactly what I'd said. He, however, had interpreted my straightforwardness as my trying to tell him what to do, as my trying to run the diocese. I have to admit this interpretation was true. Some priests are good at manipulating their bishops. I was never patient or subtle enough to do it successfully. I was too liberal, too much into the gray areas of life. Bishop Shea, on the other hand, was a right or wrong, black or white, with me or against me-type of man. So he tried to replace me, but he couldn't find anyone to take the job. Our relationship went from one storm to the next.

Shortly after Bishop Shea arrived, one of the priests who taught at Rex Mundi Catholic High School in Evansville caused a stir. Basically, he underwent a conversion experience. That priest had always been a controlling, conservative authoritarian. He used to actually beat the kids. He was that tough and frustrated. Then he heard a transforming lecture from someone. Somewhere in the late

1960s, he made a 180-degree turn in character and personality. He started preaching love and a very strong antiwar message in the classroom. He also had progressive ideas for the changes in the Church. The other teachers, the parents, and especially the new bishop "flipped out." I had to get him out of there. I transferred him from the high school to St. John's in downtown Evansville, where I had been a few years earlier. I put him together with another radical priest, reasoning that they could have at it. These two made quite a pair. Also, that central city parish, being largely ignored by the diocese at the time, was a safe move for the bishop. Eventually, though, the Ku Klux Klan burned a cross in their front yard, and once more we had to get those two radicals out of there, too.

Because of my growing interest in Father Vincent's work, and because of the struggles developing with the new bishop, I was ready to move on. My own inadequacies—feeling unwanted by Bishop Shea, turned upon by my fellow priests, and more—burbled up. I needed to search out what was happening in my life. For six months, I consulted with a psychologist in Indianapolis. I was too embarrassed and fearful of it becoming gossip to talk with someone locally. He helped me gain insight into my need for parental approval. He helped me explore the possibility of changing responsibilities, of changing jobs. He was the first to encourage me to open a door to my inner child. I began to want to play, relax, and let go.

Habits formed in the security of the job were making me feel a bit dull, too. I had told Bishop Leibold I would serve five years; my time was just about up. Bishop Leibold had already left. Now so would I. I helped Bishop Shea out by stepping down. The time spent on this job was perhaps the most interesting of times ever for such a position. It kept me on my toes. I learned a lot about self-confidence and reaching out to let others help me. Not being a teacher by trade also helped in an interesting way. It made me struggle a bit and be willing to ask others for advice which led to greater involvement. But even exciting stress can wear you down. Especially with a new bishop thrown into the equation, I was ready to move on.

My associate took the job. Everyone was happy. Poor guy. It was June, 1972. I also finally finished my dissertation that same year. Now I was a Doctor in Educational Psychology—one who couldn't quite communicate with his bishop. Bishop Shea and I could hardly ever communicate. He wasn't at all controlling like Bishop Grimmelsman, but he liked it quiet. I talked too much—and I caused too much talk as well. For example, as superintendent I felt a need to give him regular reports on the progress of schools and school activities. He didn't want reports. He just wanted things to go along smoothly. "If anything goes wrong, I'll call you," he would say, "don't call me."

I was still on the Priests' Personnel Board. One night, we got into difficulty with Bishop Shea over priests' assignments. He was ready to fire two young priests. They were part of the "new breed,"—the kind who were putting in requests about where they could go and how they wanted to work. It's common now, but it was un-heard of when Shea was young. Bishop Shea tried to say he didn't have the money to pay them. When I said I'd raise the money, he got angry with me. I was so bold as to make a few calls to some wealthy Catholics to pull together the salaries for these two. One of them must have called the bishop to inquire about the diocese's finances, because Shea changed his tune and gave the two guys what they wanted. Shea did not fully trust the new ways. Those were times of change. I accepted the realities of the new era, the diocese, the priests and the laity. Shea and I were never destined to see eye to eye.

I recall telling him once, in a heated conversation, that it was indeed my diocese, that I would be here long after he was gone and that I did have a right to my beliefs. I wasn't humble. I was vain about my education. I felt that I was better at dealing with people than he. In retrospect, I understand that he was trying to be a good bishop. All he lacked was confidence. Unfortunately, my way of interacting didn't help give him any. I was always bugging him—just by being around. When I resigned from the school office, he was so tickled. But where could I go? I asked if I could take off from June until September. Bishop Shea readily agreed.

I took a trip around the world as a reward for completing the dissertation and working in the school office all those years, for growing and learning and for putting up with the Church in general. "Well, I should have some fun." During those nearly three months, I visited friends in California, a niece in Japan, traveled alone in Hong Kong and Macao, visited a missionary priest friend in Thailand, walked the holy lands of India and the Holy Land of Israel. I cruised the Greek Isles and eventually found my way home. It was very satisfying. Once I was back, I took a look at myself. Here I was, a person with many fears, a person who didn't really like to be alone. Yet I had been alone for most of 80 days—or rather I had traveled alone. I learned to meet people and never felt all that lonely on the trip. I did hunger for companionship and would often look for people dining alone and ask to sit with them. I survived. It was one of my great experiences. I had cleared my head and was ready to come back to the whole new world of parish life. But that's not how it turned out.

Chapter 12
Learning About Risk

The extended break away from the isolation of being a pastor, first by attending college, then by working for the school office, allowed me an extended break from the traditional role of secular priest. Now it became time to return to parish life—to being a priest. Yet after all that living, I found out I could not go back emotionally and pick up from the same dysfunctional point where I had left off. The cool and controlling—artificial—priest had become a listening and more accepting human. I had faced my fears and had found love. Spiritually I was complete: embracing my male and female attributes. I found myself able to build on it. By basing my second life on need, weakness, and listening, I had a new view of life and a new attitude. Intimacy, closeness, sharing—it was unreal and it was beautiful. I came alive, refreshed and ready for a new challenge. It was 1972.

My leaving the school office made no difference in the realities of the day for the local Church. Schools were still closing in the diocese, consolidations were occurring; financial burdens were real and pressing. Among the closings was the Latin School—a prep school for the seminary on the north side of the city. The diocese's retreat center on the same campus was also witnessing decline. The Diocese of Evansville now had a huge empty building on several acres of ground. What to do with it? Unbidden, I drew up a plan for use of the center and presented it to the Priests' Council. The idea was to begin a center for the complete renewal of body and spirit for all in the diocese to use.

The council approved it. In the moment of success, I recall suddenly being unsure if drawing up the plan had truly been fortunate. In some ways, it was a blessing to have a clear plan; in others, it was a challenge to fulfill the dream. I had made my bed and now had to lie in it. Overall, I felt great about the possibilities. Great folks came on board to help. One priest lived at the Retreat House; two others—teaching priests—were installed at the old Latin School. Doris, the facility secretary, proved a great organizational asset. Together, we united these facilities for the benefit and use of the Diocese. Others came, too. We gathered teachers and leaders to create some excitement from the very real fear the Church witnessed following Vatican II and the 1960s.

Everyone who could teach taught. In the more esoteric arena, I taught a course in how to love yourself, "Love 101." We offered Scripture and religious training. We offered classes in flower decorating, painting, ceramics, typing, guitar, and more. We also had retreats—using dormitories in the old Latin School for housing. There was something going on almost every night. Sarto Center filled a definite need. The Scripture courses opened the Bible to Catholics who had never read it before. Church history, sacraments, grace—all courses proved popular and built a base from which parishes started to blossom as well. It was exciting. The Center was a magnet.

People would pull out of life for a day and come over to renew. We offered retreats for mothers, with babysitting provided. We had special religious education programs and training for teachers of persons with mental disabilities, organized by Sisters of St. Benedict. Again, I let my biological family ties slip to the background as I embraced this surrogate, supportive, complementary family at Sarto. Many of us worked and lived on site. United in work and energy—we shared meals, fun, plans, and prayer. Civic groups from the city met at Sarto. Once we offered development programs for the priesthood for six weeks in the summer. It attracted 40 priests from throughout the state. We called it Priesthood '74. It was a great renewal opportunity and a further example of the excitement of the center. The place paid for itself. And oh, how it infuriated a lot of people!

The Sarto Center worried many priests, and it worried many among the laity, too. The conservatives were being conservative: reserved, hesitant, watchful, withdrawn and, as always, scared. Change is scary. All seemed to be working out. As they say, though, no good deed goes unpunished. I had hired a young woman to work with me in running the Center. Two priest friends recommended her. My intuition was that she wasn't going to work out, but I hadn't yet learned to trust my feelings—contrary to everything I had learned about life and myself since 1967. Instead, I trusted those outside of me. I hired her. She started giving body massage classes.

I already had a coalition of priests who were out to hang me. I had laity who, still hoping for the return of Latin Masses, thought I was the Antichrist. We were just hanging on with this Center. Yes, we paid our own way—but we nevertheless worried the powers that be. We offered solid theology, but also a wider personal enrichment—something new and unusual for Roman Catholics. The priests' gossip line went something to the effect, "Jim Lex, the troublemaker, the individualist, should be in a parish like the rest of us poor bastards...." That kind of thinking was prevalent. But Bishop Shea let me go on. In short, I didn't need body massage at the Sarto Center, but once I hired the woman, I couldn't stop her. It got worse. The body massage class in 1975 was the final straw for my peers. They got together a petition to get rid of me. Petitions by your peers try your self-esteem in a big way. Still, I forged ahead. Heedless of the real risk, I hacked my way through the jungle, telling myself it had to get better. It didn't.

The younger of our two militant priests—the one who had to be shuffled out of the high school for opposing the war in Vietnam—came back into my life. As I've already recounted, he and the other radical priest down at St. John's had managed to create enough controversy to get themselves separated and moved out of downtown Evansville. It was right after the Klan had burned a cross on the rectory lawn. The personnel board got these two out of St. John's and replaced them with a very nice, caring and—most importantly—quiet priest, Father Syl. The older of our two radicals went to St. Anthony's Church, but the bishop refused to give the younger one, Father Charles, a parish.

He needed a place to live. This time, I knew what I was getting into, but I liked him. Charlie had always been a maverick priest—first as a controlling conservative, then as a zealous liberal. For example, he had gotten involved with the Black Panthers while at St. John's Parish, which is largely why he was not reassigned. Charlie needed a place to live. I had the rooms, so I told him he could come and stay at Sarto. He got into gardening in the court-yard, raising flowers and vegetables. He even built a greenhouse on the end of the building. He taught Scripture classes. The Sarto Center tamed him. And wouldn't you know it, he fell in love with a woman who had come to take classes at the Center. As their relationship evolved, they decided to go ahead and get married—again in Charlie's funky kind of way.

About six of us priests decided to attend the wedding. It was an unusual thing. We weren't there as ministers because the two married themselves. There wasn't even a license. Some time later they got legally married in Boston, where they had moved after the "wedding." On the day of the wedding, before the couple left town on their honeymoon, one of the woman's children by her previous marriage got ill and had to go into the hospital. They obviously couldn't leave with the child in there. Because they had nowhere else to stay, I let them spend the night at Sarto after they had married themselves.

The bishop got wind of it. And here it was: a priest got married (sort of), without getting permission, and I was one of those who had witnessed the wedding and, apparently, condoned it since I'd allowed them to spend the night. He saw it as a flagrant violation of just about every rule and law of the Church. So, he called me into the office the next day and exiled me. He was ready to throw me out of the diocese. He actually did throw me out of his office. He was a big, strong man with a hot temper. I didn't apologize or distance myself from my decision to be both a friend to Charlie and his wife and to offer them hospitality.

"Enough of this," said Bishop Shea, "I've had it with you! I can't decide whether to suspend you or make you a pastor." It sounded rather strange, but he said it. In the end he decided to make me a pastor. So, in 1975, at the age of 50, I was sent to St. Bernard's Church, in Rockport. My second exile; my third life. Ironically all this happened just a few weeks prior to the 25th anniversary celebration of my ordination. I had a big party scheduled at Sarto. I recall asking Bishop Shea if disciplining me meant I couldn't have my party at Sarto. He said no, it did not and I could still have the party there. He even came to the celebration and shook my hand. It's an odd world. Shea got mad, but always got over it quickly. Neither of us held grudges and that worked to our advantage in the long run.

The bishop was right. I can empathize with him now. In a Church this size, one has to follow the rules. One cannot ignore Church law—he saw that. But doesn't one have to use judgment, too? Canon law allows for personal choice, but many of its interpreters—priests and bishops—do not. Jesus obeyed the law, but he flexed the law as well. Jesus didn't always write to the chancery office to get permission. He just did the right thing. Of course, that was 2,000 years ago.

Soon after the 25th anniversary celebration of my priesthood, I went up to Rockport in the face of much publicity. The entire mess—that this priest was being disciplined—got into the local papers. Many people wrote letters in my favor to the bishop. It got a little out of hand. I can remember my mother's words the first time I was exiled, "Well, Jimmy, you know you were getting kind of cocky anyway. You shouldn't get proud and it's time you got knocked down a little." This time she gave me a little poster that says, "When life gives you lemons, make lemonade." I still have it on my wall. A paradox of all this mess was that many of the priests who were so much against me swung around to support my cause, when they saw that I didn't knuckle under or quit. A lot of priests wanted me to fight the bishop, but I figured it was no use. I was ready to go, and in 1975 I went to St. Bernard's Parish-Rockport.

I had been counseling St. Bernard's pastor for a number of weeks in early 1975 to settle some issues in the parish. He didn't want to stay there and wanted to try something else. I encouraged him to have the strength to leave that parish. The bishop had to fill the space and there wasn't really anyone else to take the post, so he threw it at me, solving two problems at once. I already knew a lot about the parish and its problems. But the entire scenario was odd. It was not your average pastor coming into your average parish. We were all in trouble. In going to Rockport, I could look back on the years at Sarto with a certain satisfaction—even as the dust settled and the explosion died down. My experience of Sarto allowed me to extend the priesthood experience beyond any parish and reach out to a lot more people.

I had learned a lot at Sarto about spirituality and taking life as it comes. About maximizing your days and continually pushing your creativity. It felt good to be at Sarto. It allowed us to take God's gifts of creation and grow with them. When I left, my friends gave me a banner that said, "Bloom where you are planted." I did. What I learned during the middle part of my life was this: I dealt with infamous bishops, irate priests, strung-out teachers, and suicidal job applicants. Each time, the temptation was to go back into my past and try to come up with the wisdom to deal with it in the absolute, one and only, unquestionably best possible way. But then, if I stepped back and thought, "Oh, to hell with it," I found that I was able to stay in the present, and that it all worked out just the same.

Balance is the trick. Staying in the present requires an exacting, delicate balance of both past and future. Wisdom requires you to be one with the moment at hand, yet still keep the ability to view the past and future without being over to either side; while staying centered in the now. The wellspring of both depression and anxiety is thinking too far ahead. I cannot control the future. No one can. With this belief, the spirituality of my gradually living towards wholeness became real.

Part III

Chapter 13
Recycling Myself

So I moved to Rockport, another small parish in a small town on the Ohio River, 20 miles east of Evansville. As with my earlier "exile" to Barr Township, I was once again supposed to curl up, die, and be buried there. Once again, it didn't work out that way. In 1975, the congregation at St. Bernard's mourned my arrival. The evening newspaper depicted me as a bad priest who had revolted against the bishop and was being sent to Rockport as a punishment. I arrived the night of a parish council meeting, which I attended. We all were tense. During the meeting, they voted five to four to build a new convent. Not exactly a ringing endorsement. There wasn't anything close to unanimity in the parish, but it was their decision. During the construction, I moved into an apartment and the sisters took over the rectory.

Right after being assigned to St. Bernard's Parish, the priests from the eastern section of the diocese—the Newburgh Deanery—elected me dean. As dean, I would be the special advocate for these parishes—an intermediary between the bishop and the parishes. My last fight had convinced them I was not all fluff and airy ideas. They thought I would stand up for them. The election was the first endorsement I had received from my comrades since my election as student body president during seminary 25 years earlier. Bishop Shea was so upset that he refused to approve my election. He attempted to change procedure and say they had to pick from three nominees he submitted. When the guys stood by me, however, and would have none of it, the bishop finally had to accept me as dean.

In Rockport, I soon met three young and enthusiastic Protestant ministers: two Methodists and a Lutheran. We shared similar struggles with life and ministry. We helped each other find our way. As the eldest, I played the bishop role in the group: the leader of the pack. We began ecumenical events and projects—retreats and social justice work. At that time, Spencer County was the poorest in Indiana. The four of us felt called upon to do something about that statistic. We were full of ourselves. We were *so* holy.

So we planned to open a little clothing store—like the St. Vincent de Paul stores, but as an ecumenical group. Then we thought, well, maybe that's not enough. We thought some more. We didn't want to be just a group of do-gooders patching holes. So we began a discernment process to find the root causes of area poverty. We spent extended time examining the entire problem. We met weekly to pray, talk, and study the Scriptures. Our first task was to identify the poor. We sat together, ministers one and all, and tried to write down a list of every poor person we knew. But we found we didn't know any. We were too removed from the poor in the community to know their problems. Through friends we found a couple of outspoken "poor" women. And they taught us about the poor. They received welfare and struggled with jobs and homes and family. Listening to them was painful, but it was such a good lesson. The process went on—talking and Scripture, talking and Scripture.

We came to the conclusion after four or five months that we were the problem. In the end, we were do-gooders out trying to save people instead of helping people decide for themselves how to grow. Honest appraisal showed that we planned to tell them what to do. It was humbling to arrive at that conclusion. The improved result of this effort was the Rockport Recycle Center. Its goal was to recycle everything: housing, clothes, cans, paper, ourselves, our neighbors—everything. There was no money to hire anyone, so we had to depend on volunteers. Gradually, the site became a resource for welfare recipients to come and get help in pulling themselves up again. It even involved health services after a while. Eventually we even raised enough money to buy a building.

The project attracted several other remarkable people; Sisters of St. Benedict Patty Lasher and Jackie Kissel came specifically to help start the Recycle Center. Jackie and I had been together at St. John's in downtown Evansville. We were an unbeatable team—we Methodists, Lutherans and Catholics. Working with these diverse ministers provided beautiful opportunities. Our friendship bore witness to the community. We socialized—dinners, ball games, and whatnot. Our friendships brought Rockport together and gave the entire community pride in what had happened between the churches.

We also started a community college. The Sarto classes were so successful that I suggested we try classes in Rockport. We persuaded key community leaders to endorse the idea; we began offering courses at the high school in the evenings. We offered the Scriptures, taught typing, writing, and all kinds of music; we also offered sports—even taught older people how to play volleyball. The various classes caught on surprisingly fast. They provided an evening's diversion. Rockport was a small town; people wanted to get out and do things.

I was coming back to life again. On the parish side, other projects took root as well. When initially assigned to St. Bernard's, I served as priest-pastor without an associate. Before too long, though, I found one on my own. My roommate came in the person of Father Tom, who had retired from a nearby parish during the winter of 1976. He was a lonely guy. He had big plans, but they had fallen apart, and he was in danger of falling apart as well. When he retired, he fairly fled the diocese. He made a great ceremony of leaving. He filled a cooler with snow, put it in his car trunk, and intended to drive south until he found a kid who didn't recognize snow. There he would stop. He got to Florida, but I doubt he ever found the kid. He stayed there two weeks; then he came back. Tom was lonely—lonelier than anyone else I have ever known. He showed up at my door one day and said, "What should I do?"

Tom had first tried to get the Little Sisters of the Poor to take him in as a resident priest, but they didn't want him. Someone had told them that he was a troublesome alcoholic. That was true. Tom did have a well-hidden problem with alcohol. But it was still a sad thing that he got told on like that. Because I was living in a small apartment, I couldn't help until the nuns moved out of the rectory. Tom floated around for a while, but not too much later the convent was finally finished and I moved back into the rectory. Tom came with me. Together, we struggled with his drinking. He was going to AA meetings in another small town nearby. He enjoyed them and was energized by the group. Tom decided to start a group of his own, which was not a good idea. He was so excited about it. No one came. He got so disgusted that he started drinking again. And smoking—he was an addict all the way around.

After a while I got to worrying that Tom would burn the rectory down. I made a rule that he could only smoke in his den. In the den, I put down fireproof carpet, making it his smoking room. Burn marks dotted the carpet from his accidents, but we survived. I also made it a rule that he could not drink before noon. So he got into the habit of getting up and playing a little golf each morning, then coming home and drinking after lunch. Once I asked, "Why do you drink?" "I'm just bored. There's no reason to live and it takes the edge off," he said. The edge—each of us struggles with the edginess and loneliness of our lives.

He did try to quit at times, which created as many problems as the drinking. He had the alcohol withdrawal symptoms and I had to take him to the hospital. He almost died once. It was crazy either way. We worked around it. I didn't preach to him or force him. He didn't need the fights; he was too old and tired for that. In the end, his drinking was OK. A saving grace was the newly remodeled convent where we'd go each evening for dinner. We'd take turns cooking. The sisters, and Tom and I dined with laughter and a soulful love. What great times—Tom just lit up with a support network around him. Every evening, getting close to dinnertime—5: 00 or 5: 30—he'd clean up, even put on some after shave. We had our own little family: "Dad" (Tom), "brother" Jim, and "sisters" Jackie, Patty, and Rosie.

After a couple of years at St. Bernard's, the Personnel Board asked me to move. I refused. They wanted me to go to Vincennes and consolidate some parishes there. No priest in his right mind would have accepted. And neither did I. I went back to the parish and told them, "When I came here I was sent, but now the bishop has asked me to move and I've refused. Now I am here of my own free choice." St. Bernard's had helped me heal again. It also allowed me the chance, at the start of my third life, to act on my longtime fascination with boats.

Rockport is a little river town on the Ohio River, a waterway integral to the town and its history. I began looking around the docks and found a boat under construction in dry dock. It was an unreal find. The man who had been building it had been forced to stop due to illness. I looked at that boat a lot—longingly, covetously—but I didn't know the man. Because he was sick I didn't want to bother him about the boat. But then he died, and this half-built boat was just sitting there. I saw in the paper that the boat was for sale.

I bought it for $1,500. I was just like a kid. The boat was 50 feet long and about 13 feet wide, with both an upper and lower deck. It looked like a trawler without the super structure. It was great. Even before its first launch, the boat became my love affair. Being on the river was timeless and calming. The lapping of the water near the dock as we worked on the boat fairly called me to come and play. With my dry-docked boat, I found love and gave loved unconditionally in return. Working on my boat was my gatherer of friends, my party to enjoy.

I got lots of teasing about it as well. Once, when it was sitting in dry dock, someone came up at night and put a pen around it and some animals in it and put a name on the boat: *Lex's Lark*. We finally did get it in the water, which was no small task because it was a big boat. We got it in the river, but we couldn't quite get the motor to work. We left that project for another month.

By this time, I had been at St. Bernard's for five years. Religiously, Rockport helped me get back into the mainstream of the Church; at Sarto I had gotten a bit outside the Church. I had done a lot of spiritual and personal roaming. Getting back into parish life was good. I renewed my faith and found a lot more love in my life. The sisters, Tom, and the Protestant ministers made it a healing place. Rockport was time well spent. After these five years at Rockport, I felt that I had redeemed myself with Bishop Shea. I had been the good priest and had done everything right. We had gotten comfortable with each other again. I thought this was a good time to request a sabbatical. I figured, after the passage of time, he might feel a little bad for the way he had treated me and he might just see fit to let me have six months off. I was exploring so much change and variety. I felt I needed to sit down and think this third life through a bit. Sabbatical programs offered places and courses to go for renewal.

So, I asked him for the time off, and he said yes. He may have been glad to get rid of me for a while—I still made him nervous. I also believe he found some joy in being able to give me a perk. I got six months. The diocese policy was to pay only for three months. He said I was on my own for the additional three. I planned to study for the first half, and meditate, cultivate and sit during the second half.

Chapter 14
Acknowledging My Intimacy

I left Rockport in 1980 for the three-month part of my sabbatical at the University of Notre Dame. It was a good renewal time for me. After my experience in the 1960s, I enjoyed having a healthy positive experience at Notre Dame. I got a better sense for the college, the Holy Cross Brothers, and the courses this time around. Studying mini-courses on theology, morality, Scripture, I met priests from all over the country—all of whom were a little calmer by this decade. I formed several close friendships.

What I found out at Notre Dame was that, I was getting overwhelmingly tired. I had been a priest for more than 30 years. The time to start wrapping things up at home—mostly my emotional baggage and lost loves—was rapidly approaching. In essence, I was five years into my third life, and its direction would include retirement and, at long last, time for me. But what did I want to do from here on out?

When I had gone to Notre Dame for my sabbatical, I'd left the boat in the river. I had arranged that some friends would take it out before winter. They came to pull it out and take it home, but in taking it up the cable broke, and the boat fell back in the water. They left it sit there overnight—to try again the next day, but during the night, though, it sank. It was a sad state of affairs. They called me up at South Bend and asked, "What do you want us to do with your boat?" "What do you mean?" "Well, it's on the bottom of the Ohio." Such is life and death. "Well, it's OK. Try to get it out as best you can." They did, but the boat was extensively damaged. After my sabbatical, I salvaged enough of it to sell it and buy another boat. You get boating in your blood. I was like a little kid with a toy. I kept coming back to boats in these later years because boats filled in parts of me that were missing—that little kid who enjoyed playing with boats, running around, and completely wasting time.

I had known for quite some time that I had to respond to the little boy in me, to let myself grow—and to let *him* grow up. I never got to be a carefree child because of Daddy's death and the seminary. My time for hanging out and having fun was cut short—I skipped over adolescence. While still on sabbatical, I nurtured my "inner child" by looking for an experience in the second three months that would offer adventure—maybe pirates and superheroes, maybe islands and ocean. I followed up the study at Notre Dame with an extended guided retreat. I knew I wanted to head south, because the three months at Notre Dame ended in December. I had called the St. Augustine Benedictine Monastery in Nassau, The Bahamas, and requested a 30-day retreat. The Abbot accepted me. So, from late December 1980 through January 1981, I stayed at the monastery and worked in the garden. Each day I had a spiritual direction conference. One of the areas I pondered over was my psyche. The "female"—i. e. emotional—side of me, and my macho side, my desires for entertainment and adventure. I began to see how I had led distinct, compartmentalized lives as I aged. I had my priestly life—and I had experienced a separate, intimate life, as well.

For a priest to admit openly that he is intimate confuses many people. Society has a definition of intimacy that is strongly sexual, but intimacy is deeper than sex. It is unity in mind. It is being vulnerable. I hadn't publicly admitted these feelings, because until the time in Nassau I was still exploring them myself. I was still carrying this big secret about my time with, and attachment to, Maggie and others. I was 55 years old, and the emotional part of me was just now coming out and demanding to be expressed. I felt guilt over my handling of earlier relationships. If ordinary folks knew what I had felt—what would they think? My need for intimacy could look like infidelity to my commitments. It was infidelity. People would probably have run me out of town. Fortunately, they never knew—until now.

Even the little that people did know about my relationships had caused concern. One time I had taken one of the sisters at Rockport to a movie. I received an anonymous call: "That was shameful," the chastising voice had whispered, "You shouldn't do that. You should never be seen in public like that." The laity demanded isolation. It's a tremendous and unrealistic burden. I forced myself, with my spiritual guide, to look at all of this. My transformation was as strong as the experience with the group in Niles more than 15 years earlier. Again, I chose to remain a priest. Finally, gratefully, painfully, I came to grips with fidelity and what fidelity meant. Fidelity usually goes unexamined in the solitary life of a priest. In a marriage, you have two people and those two will discuss with each other what fidelity to the relationship is: what is acceptable; what is not. Through discussion, they come to an agreement. In the priesthood, the priest controls both ends of the discussion. If he isn't careful, he can either be too strict or too free. That discussion was my struggle. Oftentimes, I was too free. At other times, I was too strict. Guilt, tension, overwhelmed me. I had to find a happy medium. Who had ever heard of moderate fidelity? No one is 100 percent perfect. No one is 100 percent loyal all the time. We can try, as long as we are gentle with our failure.

The laity, hierarchy and even agnostics of the world expect 100 percent faithfulness, 100 percent isolation from priests in regard to having emotional lives. It's OK if a priest drinks too much or gambles or whatever. It's just a commitment to love that is taboo. Neither is a commitment to struggle condoned. No reaching out to others. And most definitely, no touching.

In Nassau, I consciously began to decide upon who and what I would be faithful to. Was I faithful to my journey or to filling the expectations of other people? Was I faithful to growth and struggle? My breakthrough was in being certain that I knew what was best for my spiritual journey. My fidelity was to stay with my commitment to the Church, while being willing to grow and struggle. I would only be content with intimacy that I could find within the priesthood. Now that's kind of strange coming from a priest, and most people would judge this thought process harshly. But I am honest. I struggled with my feelings about Maggie—I had never reached a healthy closure to that relationship. I examined what I still felt and admitted that I'd never stopped loving her. I'd taken chances by continuing to visit her all these years. Why this fidelity to seeing her? Why this vague but persistent commitment? I had skirted these questions for years. I had hoped the feelings would just go away. Feelings *never* just go away. When I returned, they were there waiting for me. Finally, I had to deal with them. My unrequited love for Maggie carried me through to this enlightenment even in my denial. After I acknowledged that I loved her but had chosen the Church, I stopped denying the feelings. The passion finally left. The beauty of Maggie's and my friendship enlightened me.

From this retreat forward, I began to admit that I needed emotional intimacy. I had sickened of this double public and private life. The private life gave me energy. The private life told me I was worthwhile. The private life told me I was a good person. It told me I was really faithful and committed. Even though I didn't do everything everyone expected of me, I was going in the right direction. Therefore, the private life had to be embraced. It was nothing to be ashamed of. Three weeks into the month in the Bahamas, the Benedictines asked me to help at one of the small island parishes because the priest was ill. I agreed to fly over to Eluethera. Once there, I took a taxi to the harbor's edge and took a boat taxi across the harbor to this little island, three miles long and half a mile wide—Harbour Island. As I was approaching the island, I had the serene feeling of coming home; this tiny place was where I was meant to be. Harbour Island felt like my place. I claimed it that very first day. Like a little kid, "Oh, I found an island and it's mine."

After I had said the Masses and returned to Nassau, I offered to return and live on Harbour Island until the priest recovered. I had a few more months of sabbatical time after the retreat ended and really nothing else to do. So I went back to Harbour Island and looked after the needs of Blessed Sacrament Parish for the next few months. Harbour Island offered me the opportunity to absorb the island mentality. I gradually learned to live in the present. I learned about hanging out. Everything in the islands is about joy, one day at a time. There were so many people in both Nassau and Harbour Island to just hang out with, walk with, talk with, and relax with in a very deep way—different people in the habit of living in tune with the islands. Each day began with a walk on the beach. I took up painting and learned to paint watercolors. All my kid stuff. I was immediately drawn to fixing up, painting, and adding shrubs to the church property. It was another experience of love.

After I returned to Indiana to work, I began spending my vacations down on the island throughout the 1980s. When there, I worked at getting the rectory and church into shape. The priests from Canada and the nuns from New York had left by 1976 to return to their homes due to shortages of vocations and demands up north. The parish house sat vacant a lot while the islanders built up feelings of abandonment and resentment. Promises had been made and broken. For example, that the school would be continued—it hadn't been. During my first two years of short visits there, I felt that all I did was listen to people complain. Complain about losing the school. Bemoan how they hated to lose the school. Tell how they had been tricked by the bishop and cheated by the Church. While there, I listened as best I could and then I, too, left them to go back to my diocese. I longed to be able to give them the attention they so richly deserved from the Church. But all that takes time.

After the sabbatical, I was assigned to Corpus Christi Parish on Evansville's far west side. I was there from 1980 through 1984. I became familiar with death during those long years.

Chapter 15
Becoming an Orphan

In the winter of 1982, I had an opportunity to go sailing with three priests who were seasoned sailors. I had never been sailing—and I loved boats—so this was an exciting opportunity. We were an interesting group, because these were not men I usually hung out with. I ended up being the cook. We went out snorkeling in the Virgin Islands. The four of us were just off St. John—a special beach because the island has an underwater museum to see the coral. We decided to drop anchor and snorkel our way into shore. We were about 200 feet off shore. I got in the water last. While getting in the water I somehow inhaled salt water. It is very difficult to do and I don't know how I did it, but I did. Did I bump my mask? Or was water in my mask at the start? I don't know.

My body started reacting as I was swimming in. It wanted to reject the salt water and it started putting more fluid into my lungs. First thing I knew, I couldn't breathe. I tried to call out to the others, but I couldn't seem to yell. I was still quite a way from shore. I thought I was hyperventilating and tried to float on my back to calm down. But I still found that I could hardly breathe. When I was about two-thirds the way to shore I just wanted to give up. It wasn't worth the trouble. I was hallucinating a little—I told myself that it was a good place to die. I was ready to go. Then suddenly, something jerked me back to reality, and reality said, "You don't want to die here. No one knows you here." I guess there was enough of that Irish fear of looking stupid, that good old Irish grandmother training, that I swam some more and didn't give up. I got to shore, but I couldn't stand up. I lost all my muscle control. I even lost control of my bowels. It was god-awful.

A nurse just happened to be swimming at this particular beach. She saw me. She pulled me out of the water and she thought I was having a heart attack. She got a lifeguard, who just happened to have a walkie-talkie, and he called the first aid station. Fortunately, a doctor, who had just happened to forget his cigarettes, had gone back inside to get them. Within a minute there was an ambulance there. They put me on a stretcher. By this time the other three men missed me. They came over, saw the commotion on shore, looked at me and thought—each one of them—"He's dead." They identified me. The ambulance personnel took me to the aid station, where I received some oxygen and all kind of pills and medication. The doctor tested my blood and found that I had less than two percent oxygen in my body. They rushed me by boat ambulance to the hospital at St. Thomas. I was anointed. I thought that was it.

Gradually, though, I started to feel better. I wound up in intensive care—but I was alive. I was there for a week. During my stay, the hospital mixed up my medicines—another near-tragedy! I had a doctor from India who could barely speak English, the nurses and aides were all foreign to me, I couldn't understand anything they said, and I was scared and confused and frightened. The nurses couldn't give me a bath because the movement would cause stress on my lungs. It was quite an experience. Still, it got better. I was moved into a regular room—with six other guys. No magazines, no papers, no TV—I had a lot of time to think and pray. I was praying daily to understand why the drowning, the saving, and the treatment in a foreign hospital had happened. The coincidences were just too much: The doctor being there. The nurse being there. The doctor said two more minutes and I would have been dead.

"Why, why, why was I to live?" It must be for a very important reason because God went to a lot of trouble to keep me alive. For four or five days, God said nothing. Then finally one day He said, "Yes, there is a reason I kept you alive. It is so you can keep doing what you have been doing. Just live your life the best you can." I was disappointed; I didn't want to hear that. I thought I was to do something famous or something very special like Bishop Fulton Sheen. All God seemed to want of me was for me to be myself. That was some horrible lesson.

Upon my release, I returned to the boat. With the other three priests as supportive friends, I slowly learned to swim and snorkel again and not be afraid. Eventually, this drowning experience gave me a great sense of freedom. I began to see that I was *not* in charge. Perhaps the message from God was in the drowning, not in the saving. Once we come close to death, we enjoy the spiritual aspects of life more. I can try to stay in the present and enjoy God's daily gifts more. It may be all I have.

God had many lessons for me during that period. Death still pursued me. In the fall of 1981, my mother had become ill with terminal cancer. I took care of her. I became a parent, with my mother as the child. I finally grew up as I celebrated final times with her. Despite her lifetime tragedies, my mother was a happy, witty, positive, active woman. Since my youth she had been both mother and father to me. I had never been able to imagine what I would do when Mother was dead, but here we were at death's door. She was 81 years old and had intestinal cancer. She emphatically did not want to go to a hospital. I had heard about hospice. It fit her desire to stay home. Hospice meant we accepted she was dying: this was terminal. It was a hard thing to say out loud, but we did it.

We siblings invited hospice in to help. This action meant that one of us had to move in as well. Mother had to have round-the-clock care. For a variety of reasons, no one else was able to give her the care she needed. So I said I would do it. It was my choice. My friends said I was crazy; a priest just couldn't do that. Nevertheless, caring for my mother was what I needed to do. I remember telling more than a few people that if Bishop Shea were to say no, I would quit the priesthood. I could have easily left for Mother's sake. The bishop did say yes, but also expressed concern over who was to take care of the parish. I promised to be there on the weekends. We arranged that I stay with Mother throughout the week and my sister Dorothy stayed with her on the weekends.

Nurses taught me what to do—which was everything. I was in way over my head, but I never thought too far ahead and I got through it all. I learned how to get rid of her pain. I learned how to give my mother a bath. I learned to wipe her butt. I cleaned out her open cancer sores with my rubber gloves. I recall learning that to tend open sores, one of the most comfortable and useful things is a sanitary napkin. I had to go to the grocery and buy these things. Here I was, a big-time priest going to the store weekly to buy maxi-pads. I learned to give my mother opium suppositories. I learned about the TENS unit that, when applied to her back, would use electronic currents to cut off the pain produced by the cancers in her stomach and intestines. The shocks helped.

All along I wanted the various doctors to be God. It was to the point where they would hide from us. We pressed and pressed for concrete, factual information. One told us that she'd live six months. And she lived one and a half years, dying in 1983. She lived through two Christmases. The doctors' prognoses taught me about the dangers of looking into the future. I felt inadequate, felt that she would be better off in the hospital. But the nurses told me—taught me—that this was much better care than she could ever get there. I did it. I kept the records and did the reports. I cared for her.

The nurses encouraged me, but week by week, day by day, she died a little bit more. She slept in the bedroom next to mine and would wake up at night and start to yell, "Jimmy! Jimmy! Jimmy!" Oh, God, she's dying, I thought. I'd get up and go in there and she'd say she just wanted to see if I was still here. She did that often. Finally, she started getting out of bed herself. I had to sleep on the floor next to her bed so that she'd step on me. I was able to give back some of the things that Mother had given me. I fed her and looked after her. To share her death with her was one of the greatest experiences of my life. It was powerful.

She stopped eating, and I tried to force feed her. The doctors had said that starvation would finally kill her, so I had to quit trying to make her eat. She died in July, 1983. We held her wake at Little Sisters of the Poor. This was the place where she had volunteered, that she had loved. I learned again about letting go and staying in the present. Through caring for her, I had learned to let her go. Dealing with her, the doctors, my family, and myself was a journey on many levels. The "inner child" had grown, and was now an orphan several years into the beginning of another new life. The experience gave me balance—it added to what I lacked.

After Mother's death, I was able to get a little money with the settlement of the estate. The money settled an area where I had long had a concern. I was always worried that if I left the priesthood I wouldn't be able to live on the money I had. It was a loose end: I didn't have enough faith and trust in God to depend upon Him. I felt much better with money in hand, because I now knew that I was no longer beholden to others for funds. It was even more out of free choice that I could decide whether to stay or to go. I was not totally clinging, however. I had been instrumental in reducing that anxiety for priests. I had helped the diocese develop programs to get retirement benefits. The policy became fact so that retirement at age 65 was available.

I had always been afraid I would leave. Even though I had decided long ago that I would never leave while engaged as an active, working priest. Yet even into the 1980s, I held onto the option that, after I retired, I could be married. If I was going to live and work on these lonely islands, it might be handy to be married. I had it written into the policy that the retirement money could not be taken away from a priest if he left the ministry after 25 years of service. Retirement was assured whether one was a "good" priest or not; retirement was based on years of service. If a person served, he got the money.

It always feels good to know one is not staying in a relationship—a marriage or Holy Orders—just because one cannot leave. With the money from my mother's estate in hand, all my options were open. During my sabbatical and Mother's final illness, I got more insight into my many spiritual and internal issues. My near drowning and my mother's death were additional strong lessons. I began to write and write and write—about weakness, emotions, and philosophy. I got to know death and began to see that my time might be coming sooner than I thought. That would be OK. I was becoming more and more satisfied. I was learning what to pack, learning how to let go of my baggage.

Chapter 16
Going Back to the Marriage Full-time

After my sabbatical, at age 56, I finally lost my fear of quitting—of "divorcing"—the Church. At this very same time, Maggie got a divorce after 15 years of marriage. I was dumbstruck. Could this be my second chance? Was I willing? Was she? I wasn't ready—I didn't want to give up the priesthood. It turned out she wasn't ready either. But the event, the timing, the chance, gave me the closure I needed. Finally, I could let go of the hope. I turned back to my marriage. I redevoted myself to my original commitment. Only more recently did I admit to myself that I have probably *truly* been married to the Church all along. I didn't even know it or recognize it. I didn't want to admit it because to my ear it sounded silly. Yes, I was willing to serve and be part of the Church, but the whole bit about being married to the Church was not what I was interested in. Despite that, I obviously must also admit that I was married to this somewhat (often justifiably) jealous partner.

I learned to just "be" as a priest—to offer my vocation as a witness to others. Just as a parent would do, a very real reason I chose to remain a Roman Catholic priest was the obligation I felt to all those I had given sacraments to. They were my offspring. My quitting would affect their faith. When people are given instruction by a priest, they expect a certain amount of fidelity out of that priest. I believe, and continue to believe, in the Church enough to hold onto my role within her for the sake of others. Am I living an obligation rather than a positive choice? No. I have followed my vocation as a positive choice ever since the training session in Niles. I make this choice daily in my recognition and reaffirmation of my commitment. My concern has turned to the thousands of priests in the world trying to live the same commitment. The laity is blind to the level of unswerving, relentless, soul-crushing fidelity they expect. They do not know how traumatic this journey is for most priests. They do not take time to discover what struggles and fears exist inside their pastor's mind. They do not understand—and so cannot truly love—their pastor. Lack of love may be the part of the iceberg that's underwater—but the visible part is the political agony of a parish priest.

In 1983, when I returned full time to Corpus Christi Parish, I rediscovered an ongoing problem with a staff member. She was a carryover from the previous pastor, and I'd previously overlooked her while working through Mother's illness. Instead of getting rid of her, the predecessor had himself left the parish. This person was a manipulative controller and had alienated everyone, so I made up my mind not to renew her contract. She threatened suicide. She threatened to embarrass me. She sent out letters spreading false rumors.

It was a difficult time. Finally, people began to see through her—she had manipulated them and their children so skillfully that it was difficult, but eventually they supported me. She ultimately had to accept the inevitable. Interestingly, she was a nun, which really made the matter worse because her whole community didn't understand what I was doing. Yet some of the other sisters gave me encouragement and spoke to the community on my behalf. I struggled quite a bit, but finally it worked out. If you hang in there you can usually survive. That's part of life. It's part of the struggle.

Priests receive no training in how to deal with personnel issues, financial planning, taxes or fair labor laws. These issues in parish life, coupled with isolation, drive priests to distraction. It was easier—not better, but easier—in the old days when the priest was the absolute parish monarch. What he said stood and no one offered options. Many of us are still not comfortable with parish councils or personnel boards. Committees only complicated the issue and many priests didn't have the personality skills to handle a committee. The frustration of not feeling confident in how to do things can make one bitter. Until my mid-50s, I thought the bitterness was mandatory. During this time, I talked to a nun who worked in an area hospital. "I should just quit while I still feel pretty good about myself," I said, "because it looks like it's inevitable that when we get old, all priests become crotchety old bachelor bastards. There's no sense staying in and causing all that grief. I should get out now with good taste and with friends," I whined to her.

106

She made arrangements to take me to a retirement home for nuns. She pointed out many nuns sitting around the great room. "See that sister over there, she's kind, loving, thoughtful and patient, a beautiful person. She's 94," my friend said. "See that one over there. She's a witch. She's griping about everything. She doesn't like the way the elevator works. She doesn't like the food, the chairs, anything. She's 91." She went all around the room, pointing out the good and the bad of all these sisters. "Why are you telling me this?" I asked. "Well, I am telling you this because I know all of these sisters and I know that 20 years ago they were just like this. That lady was a witch 20 years ago. She was a witch 30 years ago. This lady was lovely 20 years ago and 30 years ago. Getting old is not going to change your emotions," she said. "If you were going to be griping and whining, you'd be doing it already. It's how you are and how you grow throughout life that matters."

That episode was an awakening, because I'd only known one or two old priests who were halfway decent human beings. Most of them were self-seeking bastards, focused inward. I guess they all started out that way. Perhaps it is the error of being 100 percent macho—of only exploring the male side of life. I thought anger was inevitable. But I learned.

By 1984, I had been at Corpus Christi for four years. I was looking for a change. The school created pressures that I constantly had trouble coping with. An opening at St. John's Parish in Loogootee would be coming up. My old stomping grounds from 1960. It was a long way from Evansville. The priest was leaving for the military—maybe even leaving the Catholic ministry altogether. No one was sure. I was interested in this Irish-heritage parish. It didn't have a school. I was ready for this to be my final parish. Because I was still on the personnel board, I was able to get the assignment.

Basically, it was a single priest parish in a small, mostly Catholic town. The town was the parish and the parish was the town. It was conservative, white, middle class, and middle American. Surprisingly, it was a challenging place. As it turned out, I did my best work at Loogootee. All the ingredients, young and old, no school, no burden, many people who were ripe to move. It was just that the

107

people didn't realize yet how great their potential was. I met most of the staff at a meeting soon after my arrival. They had heard of me and they had mixed feelings about my mixed up history. I began to talk about my dreams for the parish. They all were smiling and I felt great: We were off to a great start. What a nice bunch of people, I thought. Well, beginning a few days later, one by one, they came in requesting written contracts; they wanted ironclad agreements for their job security. I felt so sad that they didn't trust me.

Still, I recognized that I came across too spontaneously and off the wall. I must have scared them to death. So at our next meeting, we sat down and had a Myers-Briggs personality test. We found out that I was the only extrovert in the group. My verbal idea sessions worried these internal thinkers who didn't speak until the matter was settled. We found from the test that the staff comprised people who are attached to stability and needed time to think. I throw ideas around like a salad. We decided to publish agendas for each meeting so they would have time to think things through. After that, we got along famously. Now just to keep things interesting in Loogootee, I also wound up with a situation where the priest who was leaving never quite left. He stayed in Loogootee and hung around the parish waiting to get into the military. It was awkward having two pastors of one church. Eventually he joined the National Guard, which was good for all involved. In fact, he went on to become an Episcopalian priest and got married. Interesting.

I knew Loogootee would be my last assignment. I was retiring in a few years. While there, I could either cool it and go out with a slow glide, or I could go out with a determined uphill push for the parish. I had ideas, but at my age and with this parish, I was unsure of how to direct them. So, I hired a personal consultant, Ted De Fries, to come into the parish and help me decide what I wanted to do and what should be done. Ted came in and sat with me morning, noon, and night for two days. What a nag! He kept asking me "What do you want to do?" "What do you want to achieve?" "What are your goals?" Pulling out my goals and desires hurt. I responded that I wanted to be a good priest; I wanted things to work well. I skirted the questions. He pushed "What do you want?" Well, at that moment I wanted to kill the guy. I wanted him to go home. I wanted him to stop. Because he pushed me, instead of punching him, I wrote a personal mission statement of what I wanted to be for the parish. "I want to be the leader. I want to take them places where they want to go. I want to be a facilitator to show them how to achieve their goals." Once I saw that statement I began to look at what needed to be done.

I first took it to a personal level. I gave the parish a face—one person at a time. To do that, the staff and I divided the community on a map. We visited every parishioner, went from house to house. Along with that, we needed a parish council. We needed a program to develop lay ministers. We needed a new building for religious education. We needed to expand parking. Those weren't just my ideas; we worked as a community. The parish wanted to offer dinners after funerals. We set up committees and we found people who had never volunteered before signing up. It didn't just happen automatically though. First, we placed a sign in church for volunteers to help with the funeral dinners. No one volunteered.

The staff met and targeted five people to be chairpersons for each meal. We called them and they all agreed. And those five went through the list, targeting people on their committee. At every fifth funeral, one of the five groups would prepare the meal. It wasn't too much work, and everyone felt good about being able to help once invited. Going through the same process, we wound up with 400 or more people involved in some active form with the parish: religious education, visiting the sick, Stephens Ministry, funeral dinners, or any number of other ways. Beautiful. We also put out the first parish directory. We became a parish for each other and for the wider community. Our witness was strong. All of these activities and successes happened because I had a clear idea of my place and my purpose in the community. All of these things happened because Ted De Fries almost drove me nuts.

Chapter 17
Don't Plan Ahead

While I enjoyed the flow of months at St. John's in Loogootee, Harbour Island still pulled at my heart. Between the Feast of the Holy Family in January and Lent, usually in late February, the Caribbean fit into my life. Harbour Island had great potential. I began to plan that in my retirement I could help draw the spirit out of the people on that island. The small size of the parish lessened the demands placed on the priest. It was just a relaxed way of functioning. Parishioners on the island didn't share the American attitude of push, push, push for success.

I met unique folks on the island: Mary Cash the 80-year-old manager of the local liquor store, and her friend Katie. Then there were Dick and John, great company for a walk on the beach; Tom and his wife Maggie who lived next door and were in their 70s. I also met several hotel proprietors. Each time I came back to the island, they were so pleased. I felt like part of their family, a cousin coming in for a month each winter. I found the attitudes liberating. I could come and go as I pleased, I could do what I wanted to do: I could get up when I wanted to, say Mass when I wanted to—I was free at last! And I was praying more.

Despite its three-mile size, the island had several churches with ministers working together on several projects. We had a prayer group consisting of the Bahamian ministers and a few of us ex-patriots. We prayed for the country, for the people. Among others, I found myself joining in with The Church of God, The Church of God of Prophecy, the Haitian church. And we had a great community. At 5:00 a.m. on Thursdays we met to pray. It was open prayer. Everyone would pray out loud—everyone except the Anglican priest and me. I learned that in the Church of God everyone just prays out loud, whenever the Spirit moves him or her. So you would hear this distracting noise. It was very different from Catholic and Anglican worship. Although I appreciated being exposed to it, I could never do it myself. I was and am still too self-conscious. It seemed too vulnerable to talk to God right out loud. It seemed too awkward to listen to God speak with others at my elbow.

Most of the islanders went to all our churches. They were an ecumenical people and church was a social as well as spiritual function. I saw that the Catholic presence, the Catholic rules, mattered not one whit to these people. It was all just church. They all belonged everywhere; all the churches were God's houses. It was going well. Too well, as it turned out. I got hit with the dangers of planning ahead. After coming to Harbour Island regularly for several years, a change occurred. Suddenly the parish found a permanent priest, so I wasn't able to come that year—and maybe never could again. A group of Passionists priests had taken up presence in the Bahamas and one took the parish that I had worked so hard to improve. I had invested so much energy over several years with manual labor in repairing and stabilizing the structures and building up the parish community. But the diocese said, "We don't need you. We have a priest now. And by the way, thanks."

I let go. I went to Jamaica, to be of use for a winter. Priests and sisters on the island needed the relief help. I found another niche. There is always another niche. But just then, it turned out that the new Harbour Island Blessed Sacrament pastor wasn't working out. He made plans to sell rectory and outbuildings and buy another house on the island for use as a retreat center. He even put the property on the market. *Then* he called the bishop to inform him. Big mistake. Rule number one in the book on dealing with bishops: Call the bishop first. Bishop Burke, the Bishop of the Bahamas, came over to Harbour Island and heard the priest's story. "No. You can't," the bishop said. "If I can't, I am leaving," replied the priest. "OK," said the bishop. The priest left that day. Having finally let go, I was then called back to Harbour Island the next season to help again. I went.

One of my big discoveries during this time at Loogootee and Harbour Island was that of balance. Moderation was everything. To be moderately loving, moderately proud, moderately humble, moderately honest, moderately moderate... I developed a theory that put percentages on my life at this time. In a world that calls us constantly to be good or bad, black or white, honest or dishonest, I found my stride when I could say with pride that I was never 100 percent anything. I might be 80 percent holy and 20 percent unholy at any given time; 75 percent trusting and 25 percent distrusting from day to day; or 68 percent confident and 32 percent timid in my actions. Accepting that we are never 100 percent anything allows us to accept all of our different parts.

Whenever you are attacking someone, you tend to resort to "100 percent" language—*always* this way, *never* that way. The reality, however, is that no one is ever 100 percent *anything*. In my third life, I grew tired of arguing, so I began to agree with my critics, but only by adding at the end of the statement a percentage: "Yes, I was stubborn 80 percent of the time." And so forth. One of the percentage statements that helps keep my actions in perspective is, "Yes, I am honest, 75 percent of the time." I have a friend who is honest 100 percent of the time. He's also very sick—75 percent of the time. By making a percentage statement, I give myself patience with myself and with others. At Loogootee, as I began to study my percentage idea, I found I was more able to be sensitive to coworkers and employees. My secretary was only 20 percent difficult. The parish was only 50 percent conservative. I was only 50 percent correct—even on my good days.

As I relaxed with my theme of moderation, God became more friendly. I spent more time with Jesus, seeing him as a friend and studying his humanity. He modeled friendship and I got to know Him as more ecumenically oriented. In my first life, Jesus was our God, our father, the magicmaker, the Church. In my second life, Jesus was an emotional man. He got hurt and angry. He was my shoulder to cry on as I worked through my emotions. In this stage of life, Jesus was both God and a friend. He showed me how to feel, process, help, and listen in whatever way I could. Through Jesus, I learned to worry less about how it would all turn out; instead, I concentrated on just getting it done. I focused on Jesus as a friend, so my prayers were friend prayers. My spirituality relaxed and became more spontaneous and friendly. Jesus needed us and needed love. He was much weaker than I had ever imagined in my youth. God needed us and made us because he wanted us to help bring his love into the world. God didn't make me Roman Catholic. God didn't make me a priest. I discovered that God made me generically. I found that it was those people and events around me that formed me specifically. I have the free will to respond, but God's hands are tied. He gave it all away by giving us free will.

Yes, God made and controls nine-tenths of everything—the rocks, trees, stars, and oceans have no choices. Animals, in a manner of speaking, have no choices. But humans have choices and that is our cross to bear. God is so weak—he depends so much on our inconsistent love. Yet he is also strong, because he doesn't let us drive him crazy. We want God to do it all and want him to do for us. All of us at some time or another would happily surrender our control to God. But that doesn't help God. God tells us, "I'm just an everyday God who loves you. If you don't want me to love you, then I can control you, but I cannot both love you *and* control you. I gave you my son, I gave you the Church, but the Church can't even accept this gift. It just gives itself back to me to call the shots— and then wants me to take the blame. I gave you the sacraments, but you don't even use them, and I am so weak and helpless that I cannot do anything about it but wait for you to learn." He is so calm about waiting. If God is love, then God is weak. It's masterful. It's beautiful.

Tolerance of infirmity is another spiritual principle, and while all the good was happening in that stage of my life, my body began to give out. I began to rapidly experience a condition called peripheral neuropathy. I lost feeling and sensitivity in my hands. I simply found that I could not handle being cold. It hurt. I went to neurologists and all sorts of doctors. Finally they told me it was diabetes, alcoholism, or syphilis. They excluded alcoholism and diabetes and told me it had to be some sort of sexually transmitted disease that I caught when I was young. Well, I didn't know what to think. So they gave me massive doses of penicillin. They did a spinal tap. None of it proved—or—improved anything. It was a tough time.

I still had extended visits to Harbour Island to buoy me. The island was warm. I felt good there. I walked and rehabilitated myself whenever there. And I prayed I would last long enough to go there on a more permanent basis. I knew so many priests—everyone has so many friends—who waited and waited to retire and then just keeled over. I wanted so much to have this time for me.

113

Overall, I was feeling great mentally, and physically I was able to compensate for the loss of feeling in my hands and feet. It could have been worse. I began to think I would make it to retirement. I continued to be busy in my sickness and in the closing months of my work at Loogootee. The parish was doing well. I became the spiritual director for the chancery office in Owensboro, Kentucky. Based on a warm recommendation, the local bishop invited me to this work. Every month, I spent one day counseling the bishop and all the people who worked in the chancery office. It was a really affirming ego boost for me.

In addition, my energies were spent guiding construction of a new parish building at St. John's Parish-Loogootee. At $750,000 it was quite an ego boost for the parish—and for me. The autumn of 1989, before I retired and just as I was ready to leave for my winter stay in Harbour Island, I went to Evansville to get a physical. Well, this time it was a little different. Because of my age, the doctor ordered a stress test. "You cannot go home. Go right to the hospital." "You are in danger of dying." "I have to go home and get some pajamas," I said. "If you go home I am not responsible," he said. So I went into the hospital directly from the doctor's office. Six of my arteries were blocked. I was in really bad shape. The surgery took place that night. My heart sank. On the brink of retirement, my hands losing their feeling, and my heart trying to kill me... I died a little. What is all this? This was not my plan.

To add to the otherworldliness of the experience, in walked Bishop Shea just prior to surgery. He approached my hospital bed. He had come to anoint me. He looked sad, nervous, supportive, and kind. He was a brother that day. I vividly recall his prayer, with his hands over me: "Dear God, please help his heart. He is big-hearted. I don't understand anything about him, but he is good. Amen." It was our reconciliation and it was lovely. In response to the bishop's prayer, God helped my heart and it all worked out. I stayed with my old friend Father Pat while I recovered. Eventually I found my way back to Loogootee to close my career. After my return that autumn as pastor, I went to Jasper, Indiana, about 20 miles away, for rehabilitation of my lungs and heart. I was working constantly for that retirement day. With only a few months to go as pastor—with only a short time more to serve as a priest at the beck and call of a diocese—I suddenly thought "Wow. I made it."

I had lived through tragedy, turmoil, death, and failure. I had experienced love, compassion, and providence. My journey had been one of continual growth. Growth kept me alive. Even when I was nearing the end of my career at Loogootee, I continued to grow. While there I learned that the more clearly you know your purpose and mission in a particular place and time, the more possible it becomes to achieve that. That parish did a lot for me. And so, following a parish going-away party right after Christmas 1989, I moved on. I had looked forward to retiring for so long. I had finished the journey.

Chapter 18
Island Priest

Retirement changed my life. The continuity and the people with whom I was constantly in touch changed. Going to Harbour Island for the entire winter, I didn't see my friends for six months at a time. It was a strange and lonely experience, but I made new friends. The trade-off in terms of beauty, time, and independence in the Caribbean was worth facing my loneliness. For six months of each year in retirement, I was back home, living at St. Anthony's Parish in urban Evansville, helping out with Masses and enjoying retirement. The parish priest, Father Earl, invited me to share his space at St. Anthony's. He and I have had a close friendship all these years. We have been able to talk about women, love, the Church, the past, present, and future in a healthy way. With Earl's help, I intentionally began to live my life the way all of life should be lived: Life is meant to be enjoyed—perhaps overdone—at times in a grandiose way—with exaggeration. I have been able to play after retirement, to do things where exaggeration and grandness are good. One grand activity was to fall in love again.

Shortly after arriving in Harbour Island for the first time as a retired priest, I met Christine. It was the winter of 1990. During the Sunday morning Mass, I couldn't help but notice the most beautiful woman I had ever seen in the middle pew. Sparkling eyes, tall, poised, perfect skin, perfect teeth, she was perfection. Her beauty struck me so that I became flustered a bit during Mass. After Mass, she was waiting for me. My heart almost stopped. She said, "Hello Father, I'm Christine. Would you like to have lunch with me?" We rode in her golf cart down to a little restaurant on the harbor. There, we enjoyed a slow lunch near the water's edge. We talked about me a little and my work on the island. But we talked at length about her work in hotel management, and about her family. She was on Harbour Island to consider taking a job managing one of the small, very upscale resorts. Well-educated, interesting, and beautiful, Christine was a powerful presence. I also quickly learned that morning that she had three teenage daughters. In her younger days she had been a nurse. Now she used her education, her wisdom, and her graciousness to manage various Caribbean resort cottages.

We finished lunch and, as she drove me home to the rectory gate, Christine thanked me for joining her, "If I dine alone, all the guys hit on me. So it was nice to have you with me to keep them away. I just want to be left alone." It was a hell of a way for a relationship to start. I was her ploy to avoid trouble—a guard and nothing more. Talk about being deflated. A couple of days later, she called me. We agreed to meet and talk. She shared with me that she was divorced and wanted to work out some issues with the divorce and the Church. We talked several other times. She accepted the island resort job. She invited me over for dinner. I met her wonderful children. She was beautiful.

I went back to Evansville for the summer. I shared my news with a few mostly shocked friends, but I was so excited about having such a close friend on the island. Then, the next fall, I went back to find her again. I shared many lovely dinners with Christine and her family. Her mother loved me. They all welcomed me into their home and into the lives of Christine's daughters and grandchildren. Although her nieces and nephews treated me a bit like an old white geek, they all embraced me and our relationship. The seasons progressed, from winter to spring, with dinners, coffee and evening chats. I became the "Grandpa" of Christine's small family. It was like heaven to be welcomed by Christine and her family. Our relationship grew and it was so very comfortable. Eventually, Christine left and took another job on another Bahamian island. When I visited her there a few times, she got a bit scared. She was a devoted Catholic and not interested in getting either of us into the rumor mill. We were just feeling our way through what our relationship was and what it meant. For me, it was much calmer and less breathless than my younger encounters with Maggie. I knew what I wanted and needed was friendship and a true companion. I knew I would keep my commitment to the Church. Nevertheless, I longed to share my evenings, my joys and inner fears with another. Even at my age, I felt that I had time, that Christine and I could go slow because we weren't going in any one direction.

I had other enriching projects, other loves. When home in Evansville during the summer of 1991, I began working on a beautiful project with Jim, my old roommate at Indiana University. He was now a psychologist living in New Jersey with his wife. He had a successful practice, and we have had a long, successful friendship. Now that we were older and had more time, we found ourselves wanting to share some of our thoughts and ideas with the world. We first began making a series of videotapes, but then our collaboration evolved into a new system of teaching emotions and an emotional vocabulary for kindergarten through third grade. The object of the system was to teach children to name their feelings, identify them, and know that feelings are OK. We also wanted to teach them that, while they have no choice about feelings, they do have a choice about actions and what they do to channel their feelings in a positive way. Children, indeed all humans, do not have to behave the way they feel. There are always choices.

After we developed the plan and the curriculum, we presented it to the Diocese of Evansville Catholic schools, and several schools adopted the program right away. We found out that it helped the teachers as well as the students. It had three components: students' feelings, teachers' feelings, and parents' feelings. From the outset, the plan was to show students how to deal with feelings and to have teachers help them accept their emotions. They would be shown that behavior was a choice. We soon found, however, that we also had to deal with the teacher's feelings. How did teachers feel when they heard what the children said? How did the teacher express her feelings? And how should the teacher behave when she heard the children sharing emotional messages? Getting the response from the teachers was the best and biggest surprise. We all learned a new approach to professionalism, because many times teachers, as with other professionals, try to bury their own feelings. We also realized in the planning that we had to deal with parents, too, so we offered a special segment for the parents as well.

We worked it out with the PTAs and the schools so that everyone was in the same ballpark. At a new school, we met with everyone right off the bat. This approach allowed the parents to trust the teachers, because some of the things they heard were very personal. Teachers had to be nonjudgmental and professional about what feelings the students shared. Likewise, parents had to be shown how to deal with information about feelings the students might share with them—how the students felt about the teachers, about other children, about themselves.

It was a mutually beneficial experience and, I believe, a good experience for the first three pilot schools. After that we offered it to all schools. Thirteen schools from the diocese joined. Our first participating teachers taught the new instructors as other schools joined in. During the process, children learned to identify feelings through cartoons and charts that we provided. Students and teachers could point to 50 different feelings. Then students learned to name their feelings and give examples of them. And finally, they learned to separate *feelings* from *behavior*. When you are mad you can pout, stomp your feet, talk to someone, fight, apologize, or do any number of things. We had to undo, even at this young age, some training the children had received. Many times we discovered these children thought that being angry was bad or a sin.

This project helped me work on my personal feelings as well. As a celibate priest, I still felt so alone sometimes. My work with Jim brought home to me the need we all have to express feelings of isolation and loneliness. For a priest this need is never resolved once and for all. I practiced on myself. I named my feelings and was able to get them out and share them with others. Once we accept our feelings, we achieve a certain peace of mind. Even this late in life, I was still learning these subtle points. As I taught, I also learned the difference between feelings and behavior. In my third life I was learning to be a well-behaved adolescent.

My work with Jim went on each summer for several years, but was interrupted when Hurricane Andrew hit Harbour Island full force in 1992. CNN showed the utter devastation of the island. My friends, the children, the parish, and the pre-school—I was terrified for them all. I thought they'd all be dead. Immediately, I flew to Florida and caught the first plane for the island after the storm. The plane landed on Eluethera and we passengers saw these huge barge boats tied up in the bay. I knew they were morgue boats from

England. I hurried over to Harbour Island by ferry. It was such devastation. The once feathery palm trees looked like telephone poles. Several buildings were gone. Most of the roofs were gone. There was no safe water. The electricity and telephones were out. But no one had died; no one was even hurt. Of course, the prayer group took credit for that!

All the churches sustained serious damage in the storm, all except the Catholic Church, which had minimal damage: God's grace. All the parsonages were still intact with only minimal damage, except for the Catholic rectory. The Catholic rectory had its roof totally blown off and was a near total loss: God's wrath. Now we knew whom God liked and didn't like; my peers on the island enjoyed that one. Using insurance money the parish rebuilt the rectory, which was great from my perspective. It became much more comfortable. Hurricane Andrew had the unexpected advantage of blowing Christine back into my life—literally. She accepted a job of supervising the reconstruction and opening of another Harbour Island resort destroyed by the storm. We began again. I served as a sounding board for her frustrations with construction and assisted with some of her personal financial decisions and plans. We were supporters, companions, best friends.

With the new construction from the hurricane damage, we felt the parish didn't need some of the facility's outbuildings any longer. We turned one small house into a computer school. I had made friends with a couple of retired computer experts who lived on the island half the year, like me. They served as instructors. They taught me, too. With others in the community, we started a veterinary clinic on site to neuter the animals on the island. The wild dogs and cats needed to be controlled.

Other beings needed some control too—as well as love, space, time, and support. This is how I got involved in the issue of drug addiction. Drugs were an oppressive presence on the island. They were flying in and they were flying out and often just hanging about. Our convent was sitting there empty. So we started a halfway house for recovering addicts. It caused consternation. People asked me to take down the sign. I would carefully keep forgetting to do it. I spent a lot of time mending human fences and bailing guys out of jail. The work was painful for me because there was such a big recidivism rate, the guys kept falling back into the habit. One time, we had three guys there. One was tall, another was short, and the third was of medium height and a little heavy. Well, if you think about it, every criminal fits one of those profiles. And so every day one would be picked up for robbery or trespassing. It was just harassment. But finally the harassment slowed and eventually stopped. No one wanted to admit there were alcoholics or drug addicts on the island, and yet the whole island itself contributed so much to delinquency and addictions. Rich kids came down with their rich parents, and bought beer and drugs and virtually anything else illegal. The market was brought in. And then the substances were there. So this is where the island children got their first taste of drugs.

Aside from rehabilitating people and property, and socializing, and giving sacraments, I had to face a lot of dead time on the island. Christine was a big career executive. Many of my other friends owned small resorts. Others had their own lives to lead, with spouses, visiting children, or grandchildren. I faced the problem of what to do with my time, with my prayer and with myself. It was a beautiful place, but I tended to be lonely inside. I devised ways to have something special to do each day, so I had a reason to get up in the morning. Otherwise, at times I might have stayed in bed all week. Monday was cleanup day after a busy Sunday. I cleaned and straightened the Church and house. Tuesday was Communion to the sick. Wednesday was count collection and go to the bank. Thursday was preschool nursery to spend time with the kids. Friday was write the sermon day. And so I managed to keep busy.

Self-pity crept in when I was lonely. Loneliness and solitude— I learned about how to deal with both and what God says to you in those times. Most of all, on Harbour Island I learned how to keep from feeling sorry for myself by staying in the present moment. The priest's trick to mental health is in staying busy. Consciously or unconsciously, priests must find ways to deal with their fear of being lonely. For me, I find that I tested myself and put myself in situations of isolation to see how I would hold up. As I went along, I got better at being alone through intentional practice: I went around the world by myself, made a secret decision to return to school, took distant retreats, and discovered Harbour Island. I have made a lot of expeditions on my own. I learned to let isolation from close friends work for me, as if it were a form of prayer.

I say "prayer" because in these lessons on loneliness, I realized how empty I would have been without God, without His guidance and help. Invariably, that realization of interdependence has liberated me and has allowed me to be present to myself and to present my incompleteness to God. By allowing God to speak to me in these silences, I find loneliness transformed into spiritual solitude. I began to see the value in solitude. If you are at peace and order, and are quiet on the inside as well as on the outside, then that is *true* solitude. It takes work. It took me three "lives" to get to that point, but I learned that we have to allow solitude to enter our souls.

So, when I got word that two priests wanted to take Eluethera and Harbour Island, I was ready to experience isolation again. Who knew what was in store for me and where that would lead me?

Chapter 19
The Second Time Around

Sometime after Easter 1995, Bishop Burke wrote me to ask if I would be open to a change. Would I be willing to leave Harbour Island, and go down to Turks and Caicos? He didn't tell me that he needed a priest there. He didn't tell me about the two guys coming into Harbour Island and Eluethera. The reason he asked was that he needed to rearrange things. It helped the new priests because it allowed them to be near to each other and offer support. They didn't want to go to Turks and Caicos. Burke was Bishop of Nassau and The Bahamas, but he was also the protector of the Turks and Caicos Islands. There had been one priest there, from Trinidad. He had left around Easter. No one wanted to go there because it is so isolated—not another priest for 100 miles of ocean. So I said, "I'll think it over."

And there we left it for several months. I didn't act on the veiled invitation—I was really very satisfied on Harbour Island. Maybe the bishop would get another idea. Then, when I was home in the States for the summer, he called and offered to fly me down to the Turks and Caicos to take a look. He even offered to pick up all my things from Harbour Island and fly them down to the city of Providenciales in the Turks for me if I opted to go. No bishop had ever been so thoughtful before. When I got the letter, I went to a friend and we looked up information on Providenciales and the Turks and Caicos on the Internet. I didn't even know where the place was. We found out that Providenciales had a Chinese restaurant, a Mexican restaurant, and gambling. I thought, that couldn't be all bad. So I called and said, "Yes, I'll go."

It all happened so fast. I had left Harbour Island in June, 1996 with every intention of going back, but when I returned in the early autumn, I packed, we had a going away party, and I left. I was testing what I learned about boredom and loneliness. I was going the next step—farther from my comfort level and all my new friends—to start again as the only priest in a nation. Bishop Burke tended to minimize the place, "There's not much to do down there....

You have a few tourists." He didn't even mention the Haitians, which made up half the country's population.

Providenciales—"Provo" for short—is not so much a town as an island. The banker is the guy who started doing banking from his house and it grew and so he built the bank. And the lumberyard was in a guy's backyard, but it grew and now he owned the hardware store. And the baker used to use his own home kitchen, but then the business grew and he built a bakery. The community had a big airport, with jet service twice daily, and lots of tourists come in on those jets.

Only after accepting the job, did I discover that I had three Masses on the weekend, with three different congregations: One in the air-conditioned ballroom of the Ramada Hotel for the tourists. That was nice. Then I had a Sunday morning Mass at 9:00 for the English-speaking people who were not staying at the hotel. Then, there was a 10:30 Mass for the Haitians. I knew I could do the Masses for the tourist and English-speaking populations, but the Haitian Mass was a different creature. The Haitian Mass is long. It is spontaneous. It is full of music. I really didn't know *what* to do. I asked a parishioner to help me out for the first week. He agreed and said he'd point to me whenever it was my turn. So we struggled through that first Mass. During the following week, he and I met and he quickly taught me to read some Creole. I learned some preliminary prayers and how to say good morning. Creole is a combination of French and African dialects. It is structured so that it is easy to pronounce and to read phonetically. So I was able to catch on quickly and within a few weeks I started reading a little more and it all worked out.

Then I started getting calls from the outer islands—remember, I was the only priest in the entire country. Others requested a weekly Mass. I wasn't aware the need existed. I guess I thought all the Catholics were on these two islands. So I began flying 75 miles over to Grand Turk, the island with the nation's capital city. There was a rectory and car, all sitting empty. The only church consisted of a small chapel in the rectory. I began to say Mass there for the English speakers. And we had a Mass for the Haitians in the larger Anglican Church. Soon we decided to build a church to fill the needs of both the English speakers and the Haitians. We received a major grant from a missionary society to build the church, because it was the only capital city anywhere in the world without a Catholic church. Rome thought it would be good and purposeful to build one. No more borrowing churches on Grand Turk. Then I started going to the Haitians on North Caicos and celebrating Mass. Soon I started flying to South Caicos and offer Mass there. It was too much for one weekend, but I was able to maintain a schedule of going to North and South Caicos every other week. It evolved to a saner schedule for me, but one that meant people couldn't have weekly Mass. Each weekend I had five Masses. I flew from one island to the next. It got to be where I had one main church on Provo and three missions.

It was interesting, but it got to be a lot of work, too. Here I was, retired and in ill health a lot of the time, and I had accepted more work than I had done in a long while. The weekends were frantic, but from Monday through Saturday afternoon there wasn't really much to do. I swam, lay on the beach, read, gardened, but really—basically—got very lonely again. I was probably the oldest person on the island. Provo was filled with upwardly mobile youngsters. It had just recently developed commercially. Twenty years earlier 500 people had lived in three fishing villages. Now 15,000 crowded the city, and it was still growing. The beauty and safety of it, the banking and speculating were good for a lot of people. It was a place on the upswing—busy. But for me, lonely. I had to do something, so I joined the Rotary Club. Rotary was good for me because it was a mixed crowd and it offered ample social time. We'd meet a little early and have drinks and dinner, enjoy the meeting and hang around after to talk some more. It was a fun night out, men and women together. After a while, my friends from the States would come for visits. I had a flow of people. Also, as I got to know the Haitians and others on the island, I developed friendships that eased the isolation. During one summer back in Indiana, I was able to procure and ship two vans to bus people to church. Several of the Haitians were in small fishing villages outside the main town, and it was four or five miles to the church. I found donors for the vans and we trained drivers. Initially, I was so proud of those vans and so protective that I didn't want anything to happen to them. But when you are dealing with new drivers, well, you just have to put up with broken taillights and assorted bumps and bends and kinks.

Then I started my sign adventure. There were no identifying signs on these islands. The town of Provo originally was something like 20 miles long, but only one road wide. As the city grew, there were more streets and lanes added. Too bad no one ever bothered to buy any street signs. You had no way to give directions using the streets. It was all based on the old-time way of saying, "Well, you know where Joe Smith lives. Well, go left there." But Joe Smith didn't live there anymore, the old bakery had closed, and so forth. The police and fire departments had a heck of a time. With the topsy-turvy growth, it was impossible to ever be certain where the emergency was. I persuaded Provo's leaders to set up a committee to study the needs. And because it was my idea, I was one of the first assigned to the group. Our first decision was to put up mile markers on the highway; we bought 350 signs to place a sign every one-tenth of a mile on the main road. These projects were such fun; it was like being a child again and building a town to play in. Soon, however, my health came calling again.

One Thursday in 1997, on a plane coming back from Mass in North Caicos, I'd noticed something odd with my vision, but the problem really hit me when I got into the car and began to drive home from the airport. I saw two of everything: there were two cars coming at me, two roads to drive on, and two steering wheels. I covered one of my eyes and slowly made my way home. I called the doctor and found that he was off Thursdays. And I thought, "Well, OK, I'll just rest. Maybe it'll right itself." But it didn't. Friday was the same, so I finally visited the doctor. He felt that I had broken a blood vessel in my optic nerve. He advised just slowing down and waiting two or three weeks for the vessel to heal. I was scared. As I mentioned, for the past several years my hands and feet had been growing increasingly numb with peripheral neuropathy. I was afraid it had now struck my eyes. And I depended so much on my sight. Without my eyes—even for those few days—I felt old and feeble and dead.

126

I went so far as to fly back to the States and make an appointment for a second opinion at the Mayo Clinic in Jacksonville, Florida. There the doctor also told me that I had probably broken a blood vessel in my optic nerve. A reassuring second opinion. This doctor, however, went a little further and fixed me up with some glasses that had a prism in them to correct the problem. It adjusted the difference. I was to wear them for a few weeks, until I started seeing double with the glasses *on*. At that point, I was to take them off and I'd be all set. What a blessing, what a great blessing our sight is! While I was at the Mayo Clinic, the doctors also discovered that I had diabetes. All along, since my health had started to deteriorate, I suspected I had some problem with diabetes, but no one could ever find it. It contributed to the acceleration of my neuropathy. I started taking the diabetes medication and felt better. I began watching my diet more and doing other exercises under the guidance of a therapist. My peripheral neuropathy got a little better, too.

It's a good thing I felt so much better, because I had a lot of work before me on Provo. A few people I met seemed to be waiting to be invited into the Church. One such person was a lady who did massage. She was a native to the island with an interest in the Church. We got to talking one afternoon and decided to swap massage for instructions, a clever idea. And later she was accepted into the Church and became one of only two black, island-born Catholics in the entire country. Most of the black population were Baptists, because the Catholic Church had not even made any efforts at evangelization in the Turks and Caicos. The other convert I was lucky enough to meet was a black farmer on North Caicos. He had been wondering about the Roman Catholic Church and had many questions. I found myself repeatedly running into him. Suddenly he started coming to Mass. He was so drawn to it. I was honored. Surprisingly, of the now three islander Catholics in the entire nation, I was responsible for two of them. I found myself giving instruction with the enthusiasm of my younger days. What a surprise.

As usual, visitors were welcomed. Several classmates from seminary came down to visit. We were lucky to be able to get a condo where we could stay all together. It was a joy to spend the time—the relaxed time at this old age—just being.

These were guys who, 25 or even 15 years before, had stood opposed to just about everything I did, said, or believed. They hadn't liked me in the school office. They hadn't liked my leadership. They hadn't liked my approach to Christianity. They out-and-out hated me at Sarto. Time had mellowed us, however. Nowadays they even quote me. If you live long enough it all comes back to you— *and* we appreciate it so much more the second time around!

Chapter 20
Recycling, Adventuring, Understanding

I have recycled myself several times since my ordination. I have recycled companions, priests, nuns, and parishes. Nothing is ever lost. There is always a way to rise from the ashes and be put to good use. My experience with people with mental problems, since my time at St. John's Parish in Evansville in the late 1960s, has led me to see the beauty in the lives of those who, due to the nature of their illnesses, are lucky enough to live in the present moment. Being closely involved with people coping with mental disabilities has, in one way or another, given me enormous happiness. They have helped me understand that each moment has the power to awe and to inspire.

For many summers, I volunteered at the Anderson Woods Summer Camp for adults with mental disabilities. The camp is operated on the premise that most disabled people, whether their disability is emotional, mental, or physical, don't get the chance for vacations. This rugged, backwoods camp, located in beautiful, secluded woods near Hoosier National Forest, offered a vacation for people with disabilities. At Anderson Woods, guests slept in bunkhouses, went on hayrides, swam in the creek, played with the cats and dogs, and sat around the campfire, singing. They also got to watch me cook—lucky them!

The camp's founder and director believed that everyone should have the opportunity for lush living and for fancy feasts of organic foods, picked by hand from the nearby cottage garden. She taught me to read cookbooks and follow the instructions. Meals at Anderson Woods were special times of fun and wonder—especially for me as camp cook. Being always more concerned with how things sound rather than with the way they really were, I am here to tell you that I cook big, complex menus. My menus include things like Kale Casserole with Blueberry Muffins Inside, or Tuna Barbecue. And if I've cooked 16 hamburgers for a dinner, it sounds more like I'd cooked 160 when I tell the story. Sometimes the camp cooks featured flaming food— flaming by intent by the way, not by accident. We've made beautiful salads, and we always garnished the plates attractively.

Camp experience was great for me, because coming back each summer from the relative isolation of the islands, I love being around all these boisterous groups of 20, 30, or 40 people. They trusted me to cook. Priests are not known to be great, or even good, cooks. They hire cooks or just eat badly most of the time. To me, cooking is gratifying and exciting. It has always been fun to see how well everything comes out. It helped me learn to trust my intuition. I even wrote my own cookbook about using leftovers, *The Recycle Cookbook*. The book was used as a fundraiser for the St. Anthony's Center for Family Life, in Evansville. We raised about $4,000 from it. Camp cooking is an adventure and for a personality like mine— it was like a bridge to friendlier situations.

Taking a long cruise alone is another type of adventure. Perhaps I feel that in the atmosphere of the cruise ship, people will be open to forging new relationships. In 1994, I took a three-week cruise as ship's chaplain, beginning at Fort Lauderdale, bound for Nassau, the Virgin Islands, Aruba, the Panama Canal, on to Costa Rica, up Mexico's western coast and northward to Los Angeles, San Francisco, Seattle, and Vancouver. I received room and board in exchange for my being chaplain and conducting Mass. Almost immediately after embarking, my search for new friends led me to the Protestant chaplain and his wife. We hit it off famously. I assisted at his services and he assisted in mine. His wife played the organ and he distributed the hymnals. They were a lovely couple from Pennsylvania, and I found myself thinking how wonderful it was that this minister had a wife who was so beautifully complementary to him that they could work together.

We had a great group of passengers. Mass did not coincide with any other onboard activities. It was convenient and easy for many people to come and venture into the room. I received a lot of energy from the passengers who came to Mass. Some of them were certainly either not Catholic, or had not been actively Catholic for some time. The scenery we passed, especially the Panama Canal, motivated my energy. I found that I prepared better, more thorough homilies. The group received them well, and the entire 21 days took on the flavor of a retreat.

I had proved to myself again that when I go out on my own, I could make new friends and strong connections. This trip was another event in my ongoing struggle to convince myself that I am lovable. What is wrong with me that I feel I have to struggle so with such feelings after more than 70 years? *Why* are some people so satisfied and so confident? *Why* am I always seeking adventure and new experiences? I guess I'll never know. But that still doesn't stop me from wanting to understand. I also want to understand other priests. I have found that in these later years I am increasingly interested in bearing witness to the brotherhood of helping priests recycle their lives—especially priests with broken spirits. By the nature of my personality, I spend a lot of time with priests who are struggling with the fallout of mandatory celibacy: alcoholism, anger, dysfunction. I share their struggle.

Through watching my friends' struggles over many years, I have felt the tremendous pain of mandated celibacy. In attempting to understand how a good, moral, intelligent person can turn into a paranoid, fearful, stunted hermit, I have extended myself to them. This extension has taken me to visit a psychiatric institution in Colorado, a prison in Kentucky, a hotel office in Pennsylvania. By seeking priests who had become ill in their isolation, I stand up for these men. I witness our friendship. I do so because *someone* must do so publicly. I am offended when the Church or other priests don't stand up for their own fallen. Give me the guy with leprosy: I will take him for a walk. One thing I have never been afraid or self-conscious about is making moral choices. I stood up for Catholic Action. I stood up for Father John. I stood up for our militant priests in the '70s. I have also stood by the imprisoned, the ruined, and the forgotten.

I recall driving from Evansville to Pennsylvania to see a friend— an inactive priest—who had been having his struggles. As I sped down the interstate, I recall wondering why I was doing it? My answer to myself was: "Well, I like the guy, and I hope he's doing OK." I simply felt that I needed to say that to his face; maybe he would believe it more easily. This particular friend is gay. His being gay compounds his struggles because he is completely honest, and is constantly telling everyone he is gay—even if no one is asking. He struggles because he has to be 100 percent correct in being gay, and he is unsure of how a gay person is supposed to behave. This attitude drives him to distraction and has created many emotional problems for him. He doesn't yet buy my percentage idea—never to be 100 percent anything. As a psychologist, I understand struggles with celibacy, sex, and intimacy. By reaching out to him and others, I can show that the struggle is OK. The feelings are OK. I have always felt a blind love for being in the community of priests. My fond memories of my comrades in seminary, of the team and the laughs, have always led me to build community first and foremost. Ultimately, I remember how much it hurts when you don't get the support you need to live. That's why I extend my friendship publicly—in front of the media at the courthouse or via the personnel board in the diocese. It's vital to have someone who is not afraid to be seen in your corner.

Although I have been dismayed by the number of priests who do not share the burdens of their comrades who are in serious trouble, I am by no means the only priest who stands up for the these men. Increasingly, other younger priests reach out to offer help and support to the men who have discovered that the yoke of the priesthood is neither easy nor light. It does me so much good to see the closeness and depth of relationship among these younger men. Thirty years ago, it would have been much harder. Possibly because there are fewer priests now, we are sticking together better. Trauma breeds changes in habits.

Time and again I ponder, "What is this word 'celibacy?'" From priest to priest, it all comes down to definitions. In the old days, before people began to talk about issues on the Internet and Oprah, murky little "things" went on, quietly and without question. One former bishop had an attractive woman as his assistant. She lived in the same house with him. You'd often see them out for dinner or at an event. Another prominent priest, one of the pillars of goodness for our diocese in the 1960s, had a housekeeper who lived in the rectory with him and you'd see them out together a lot. And today, we see old, invalid priests living with women who are their primary caregivers and nurturers. We see priests vacationing and dining with women. I find that if he is an old and ugly priest, no one minds or says much. But if he is under 60 and is active and in good health, you hear a lot of whispers. Who's to know? The invalid may be the one having the physical relationship and the young guy may just be having dinner.

Does being celibate mean you are not married? Or does it mean you do not have close, intimate relationships with anyone? Is celibacy just not having sex? I contend that the definition is as broad as the number of priests and female—and sometimes male—religious. If you look in Catholic encyclopedias, Catholic dictionaries, and in canon law, celibacy is defined as not being married. In these textbooks, the "vow of chastity" refers to being celibate. But being in love is chaste. Married persons are chaste. Chastity requires only that we do not dishonor others or ourselves sexually.

As I understand it now, the fundamental intent is for the celibate to be unattached and without persons dependant upon him or her. Despite this goal, the Church allows priests to adopt children. Are these men no longer celibate? The Church has allowed married Protestant ministers to become Catholics and ordained them Roman Catholic priests. Are *they* celibate?

In the years before my studies at Indiana University, I saw threats to celibacy as the supreme weakness. It exposes the celibate's weaknesses in a powerful way. It challenges a deep part of men and women's subconscious—the desire to have offspring. As priests and religious, we cannot have children, so we throw our energies into other kinds of offspring. We have "house-babies," "book-babies," "parish center-babies," "grotto babies." We strive to somehow satisfy that urge. In the late 1980s, I finally had my "building-baby" while at Loogootee.

We all fall prey to the building vice—the need to leave something behind. That's why so many priests in the old days used to build churches, schools, and hospitals. They were having their "babies." Today, we are left with their legacy. Current priests don't need, or simply can't financially afford, to do all of this building. That's the reason we have a large number of priests turning to other outlets in their desire for "offspring." Sometimes, finding these outlets has led to destructive outcomes.

Chapter 21
Reconciling Celibacy and Love

In any given diocese, at any time, there are priests being treated for a variety of mental health problems. Some of them displayed blatant sexual dysfunction. My question: "Why should anyone be surprised?" When you put the requirement of demanded celibacy into the mix of ministry, and if the practicing celibate doesn't fully understand or believe in the concept, then it will define his very vision of the world and affect every issue he encounters.

Emotional celibacy leads to dishonesty and lies. Healthy sexual persons who spend their lives celibate and without any sort of intimacy—"intimacy" does *not* always have to be genital, by the way— will begin to tell the worst sort of lies: internal lies. Healthy sexual persons who enjoy emotional intimacy have far better odds of enjoying good mental health, but they run the very great risk of becoming physically intimate, which leads to external lies. It's a hard maze to navigate.

I recall an encounter with a fellow priest many years ago. In the eyes of his congregation, he was a beloved and respected pastor. In the eyes of his fellow priests, however, he was dysfunctional as hell. His homilies were magnificent. He raised money with ease for his projects. Yet as a person, he was overwhelmingly dishonest. He was sick—but there was no one who cared. Not one of us cared, and we didn't lift a finger to stop him from destroying himself—and many others as well. Once, I briefly cared enough—or was I perhaps just being cruel? I'm still not sure where the truth lies—to try confronting him. In front of several other priests, I said to him, "Would you take off that damned mask?" I called him on his lies, and he was shocked. But he didn't accept my invitation. He's now in an asylum in Colorado, so very alone, and so far gone that he'll never come back to reality. I once visited him in Colorado and, for the very first time, he showed a chink in his armor. He spoke of the struggles of the priesthood. He seemed to be trying to make a statement of responsibility, but the afternoon lingered and I finally had to go. That was the last chance. He has never admitted his problem. His denial is complete.

There are other cases: the close friend who called me to say he had swallowed a bottle of pills. I fairly flew to the rectory and found him on the floor, the pills dissolving in his mouth. We had his stomach pumped to be sure he hadn't swallowed any of them. He hadn't. He took the pills and held them in his mouth too paralyzed with fear to even swallow, too paralyzed with isolation and fear to go on. At least he viewed me as enough of a friend that he called me, rather than going on to the next crisis. There are so many other examples of the cruelty of emotional distance. Often, no one has any idea whether or not a priest is off-center until it is too late. No one goes to bed at night with you and says, "Honey, you really have to stop drinking." No one finds the dirty magazine, because no one is looking through your desk for a checkbook to pay the gas and electric bill. No one really cares where you are when you leave town for a few nights during the week. Privacy can breed dangerous idiosyncrasies. Too much privacy turns the world's lies into your truth.

My definition of celibacy insists that I be honest as I share intimacy with others. I must take full responsibility for the commitments I have already made to the Church. I must also be upfront with the facts: I love you and care for you and will give you this much, but that is all. Clinically, it's interesting to hear priests talk about their innovative personal definitions of what the word "celibacy" means. No marriage? No sex? No smooching? No flirting? No serious discussions of personal issues? I have found the more exclusive the interpretation, the more problems a guy tends to have. I have also found that the laity defines celibacy much more rigidly than do most priests. I have learned to find my own path.

If an emotional need preoccupies you and is all you think about, it is a problem. Relationships have a physical, sexual, and emotional side: maybe the needs are unconscious. But Roman Catholic priests cannot explore many, if any, relationships. For a priest, there is no way to get all those needs met. Before I developed this honesty, I was a tease. Many priests remain at the teasing, adolescent, flirtatious stage for their entire lives.

It is good to be celibate. It is good to be fully committed to the marriage of my vocation. But what I see as a more healthy value is making the vow for five or ten years at a time—akin to the initial vows of a woman religious. Making a lifetime vow of chastity leads to priests who ultimately evolve as less than committed to their vow. And then the control bothers them all the time. Each time a situation with another human arises, they have to think, "Oh boy, I am in trouble." "Ok, let's just pretend everything is fine." And they cannot talk to anyone about their feelings, nor can they act on them.

If they could say, "Look, I am committed to this mission for the next six years, but after that we can create a relationship," then I believe the obsessions would evaporate—or at least be controllable. When all is said and done, what makes good priests is not the homily or the financial planning; it is the willingness to give up the time in a complete commitment to the Church and the Body of Christ. The way we seek vocations today, however, is that we look first for someone who is naïve enough to make an uninformed vow of celibacy, then to his relationship with the Holy Spirit, then we look for the value of his skills—and only after all that do we consider his commitment to the work of the Church. I look at my colleagues who have left the priesthood and I see they are all still priests. It's just that they are not Roman Catholic priests. They still aspire to serve, to understand, and to heal, but they are doing it as counselors in nursing homes, with hospice, or with those searching outside the church. They are still priests in their minds and in their actions. But with celibacy as the defining issue, they had to get other jobs.

My friend and former roommate Jim is my beautiful example. When we were students together at Indiana University, and he was superintendent of the Diocese of Evansville Catholic schools, he just didn't seem happy. He was so smart and talented—*and* unhappy. Jim was bigger than the diocese: He had great vision. Well, a woman professor lived upstairs. She was intelligent, exotic, and she was gorgeous. Once, we invited her to a party where she and Jim struck up a quiet relationship. I didn't realize how deeply involved they were. After letting go of his position with the schools, Jim got permission to go to New York and teach. After that, the separation from the diocese was complete, and he and his relationship with his wife-to-be progressed with no one around to notice. I don't recall him telling me that he was going to marry her, but I don't recall any surprise by the time the event took place. And Jim has been *much* better off.

When I mention to people how happy Jim or some other married priest is, they are shocked. They seem to disbelieve that a guy could be happier outside the priesthood. Many Catholics still believe that being a priest is the highest calling a man can have and that it's all gravy from there on in. They don't fully understand the role, the job, and the demands. The Church has many priests serving simply because it is so difficult to go through with quitting.

Celibacy—or maybe sex in general—has become a defining issue for a Roman Catholic priest. We are missing out on the fuller dimension of the Trinity and of the possibilities that would open before the Church if the issue were fully examined. Of course, being a Roman Catholic priest *does* have its perks. It is a unique lifestyle with lots of room to explore if you feel the need. Priests get attention and respect. They get automatic regard and deference. Some of the respect bloats priests' egos. Sometimes it can be downright fun.

No marriage, after all, is 100 percent perfect. Celibacy is a trade-off. Celibacy is never, ever, 100 percent satisfactory. But what in this life is 100 percent satisfactory 100 percent of the time? This life is not meant as the be-all and end-all. We have to figure out a way to live out our lives while still being as honest as we can in relationships. We have to be accepting rather than excluding.

If I can stay in the present and look at each relationship right now for what it is, and give myself to that moment the best I am able, then the commitment is not to the person as much as it is to the truth. I am searching for the truth. Hopefully, this search will bring peace and satisfaction and joy into my lonely life. After all is said and done, *truth* is why I practice celibacy. The goal is to have an enriched life, to give and be able to share, and to be able to love as many as I can.

I've spent a lot of time and training trying to define celibacy in developmental stages. I have found a natural progression of needs: 1) physical relationships; 2) social intercourse; 3) interpersonal-intimacy; 4) ego needs, and 5) clerical celibacy. The first level of need is the physical one for touch and feel. The need to reach out and touch. Lust is part of this first level, with an emphasis on the physical. When these needs are satisfied or understood, then I can move to a social intercourse with emphasis on talking, socializing, going out. This is the level when outside rules—the rumors—pinch the celibate person.

After this is worked out, comes the personal intercourse. The more intimate I feel, the more statements need to be truly exchanged. It's not just physical and it's not just social. It is a development of all the parts of both persons. You have to go through these stages to develop what can be called "clerical celibacy"—a celibacy that goes beyond ego needs. At this level, relationships seek the greater good, the common good. You have to find out what love is before you can be a celibate. If you don't, celibacy becomes a *negative* choice. When you think of celibacy as negative, it is creating a vacuum. Nature abhors a vacuum, and that's why so many people— including many priests—cannot comprehend celibacy, because all they allow themselves to see is the negative.

If celibacy is the negative of giving up something, it's not much of a gift. I have finally redefined celibacy as something positive and creative and ongoing. It is the process of seeking the good of the other—realizing that sometimes because of low tides in my emotions I could fall back and get into my self-ego needs. It is a struggle. Celibacy is a commitment to struggling. It is a commitment to honesty, to listening and to communication. Properly viewed, celibacy is an intense commitment that only limits intimacy when it is not in the priest's, nor the Church's, best interest. Properly viewed, celibacy is seeking what God calls on us to share— with an intimate love of God.

When I only see the controlling aspect of celibacy, I am not seeing possibilities for an open, communicating intimacy that moderate celibacy should bring. Celibacy requires the highest level of honesty and maturity to be able to work through the love of self for the greater good of loving others. I have to be mature to be able to accept this gift in my life. It's not human to think that accepting celibacy is ever complete. It is never final, as I remind myself often. Even today, I feel very alone after all the Sunday Masses or after a long day of work.

It would be nice to fall asleep on the couch with someone. It would be nice to be married to a person and not an institution. I am still open and aware of possibilities. Maybe someday I will meet someone, who knows where or when, and I will quit and get married. I have spent my entire life looking. Yet, I never get so deeply involved that I want to get a divorce. I want the companionship, the respect, and the trust of another human, but I also want to continue to do the priestly ministry—to be with God in an intimate way. It's a paradox and a mystery. It is difficult to share these confused emotions because the world tends to look at these things—celibacy, vocation, sex, intimacy—as either-or, as black-or-white. I struggle with trying to listen to what is in my heart and what I am called to do. The struggle is a never-ending one.

Chapter 22
I Am Trinity

My third stage of life has been much more mystical. God is in the day and in the sun and in the universe. God is transcendent and beyond the confines of any institution. God is only in the present. We pray, "Give us this day..." or "and these thy gifts which we are about to receive...." We do not pray for yesterday's bread nor do we count on tomorrow's bread. Our prayers to a present-minded God are only for today. I have come to understand that God doesn't even know what will happen tomorrow. Because we have free will, God doesn't know what we will choose. He may be able to guess if he wanted. He certainly does have good data! Still, he doesn't know for sure.

God is generic in creation. The circumstances of each life make you specific. God gave it all away. Giving us free will gives us control. God controls nine-tenths of creation—the animals, flowers, plants, seasons—but he doesn't control humanity. Yet we still want God to control things or to do them for us. Feed the hungry. Stop wars. Do it all. Humans would happily surrender all control up to God and become like the trees and the plants. But that wouldn't help God any. God is only concerned with the now. Tomorrow doesn't exist. Settling into these truths about God discourages me from too much planning. When I talk with God and ask God where I should go next, where I can serve next year, God responds, "Why bother asking. It'll just happen."

I have come to believe that with God all things work together for good. To paraphrase St. Paul, God transcends the world, but God is also of the world. Through God's presence, the world's cosmology is changing. You can feel it and wonder. We are gaining awareness that this world is God, the world is spiritual and it is precious. People who search are discovering that the world is not a mechanical device that requires fixing. The world is of God and is already perfect. The mechanical earth idea creates greed. By ridding our cosmology of the knee-jerk, fix-it, stop-it, change-it mode, we take man out of the driver's seat and place God at the center.

The world is not here for my service, the world just is, just as God is, has ever been and always will be.

God does not believe in control. Catholic conservatism or Protestant fundamentalism are based on control: this or that is bad and must be stopped, changed, or fixed. When you start with a predetermined immutable premise, the outcome itself also becomes predetermined. I stopped believing that God worked that way a long time ago. God gave us free will. God gave us choice. I don't think any rules or laws can improve upon that. "I am so helpless," says God. "I can't do anything but wait for you to learn." God's strength comes from weakness. I am formed in the image of God. I have found God through what He has given me. That's not to say He answered my prayers. This prayer is a personal favorite that I found somewhere along the way:

> **The Prayer of the Unknown Confederate Soldier**
> *"I asked God for strength that I might achieve, I*
> *was made weak that I might learn humbly to obey.*
> *I asked for health that I might do greater things,*
> *I was given infirmity that I might do better things.*
> *I asked for riches that I be happy, I was given*
> *poverty that I might be wise. I asked for power that*
> *I might have the praise of men and women, I was*
> *given weakness that I might feel the need of God.*
> *I asked for all things that I might enjoy life.*
> *I was given life that I might enjoy all things.*
> *I got nothing that I asked for but everything*
> *that I had hoped for. Almost despite myself,*
> *my unspoken prayers were answered. I am among*
> *all men and women most richly blessed. Amen."*

That really says it all for me. That is the perfection we seek. Allowing myself to grow toward these ideas and beliefs has opened many doors. Once you open the door, you see so many more connections. I now see the connections where God has been involved in my life. For a long while, God seemed very aloof. During those middle years, I often thought that I didn't care if there was a heaven or a hell, because I was living life then to the fullest. That has changed.

When I was young—until age 35 or 40, I let the Church be completely responsible for me. In my second life I took responsibility for myself and made my own decisions. Now, I am old and it's fully integrated—God, the spirituality of the Church, and me. It's good I took this long to get here, to accept the weakness of not having all the answers. Now I am free to hear God. We are all made in the image and likeness of God. If this is true, then each of us is a trinity: Spirit, Father, and Son. God has told us He is a dynamic of three beings. God exists in relation to His parts. So must we all.

The Trinity is now my focus. For the longest time I just let the Trinity alone because it was so mysterious. I didn't want to even consider it. I would rather just think about Jesus and let the Trinity be. But now, in my old age, I see three parts of me: the real me, the person I would like to be, and the relationship between these two. And when I am together with all three, I find I like myself more. I am more in union with God. The Father is dreams, aspirations, and the ideal to measure against. The Son is the human enjoyment, the temper, the physical, and the emotional. And the Holy Spirit is the dynamic between the Father and the Son. When I am less unified, I am moving away from God because I don't like myself, and I am rejecting what God has made. It's a struggle to accept myself, love myself, and share myself with others. It's a struggle to hold a trinity together.

There are constant trinities—if only we are just willing to look for them. The Church is a trinity: there is the ideal of the Roman Catholic Church, the realities of the Roman Catholic Church, and the spirit of interrelation between the two. We all see the discrepancies between the three, but that's OK. Sin offends our internal trinity. If I commit adultery, it offends my trinity as well as the Holy Trinity. If I pursue something that is not right and true, I offend both God and myself. When I enjoy the relation between reality and ideal, then I am unified with God. Our relationship with God should be a living relationship, never cemented, never the same from year to year. People change, dynamics change, and when my relationship with God is dynamic and close, it is a relationship not of this world. At such times, I am finding heaven. I look forward to being one with God in an active relationship. My heart is restless till I rest in the Trinity.

When I went around the world in 1972, I was 47 years old. While in Calcutta, India, I saw a dead baby girl floating in the river. I ran to tell the people, "There is a dead baby in the river." They looked over and said, "It is a girl." And they went about their work. I knew then and there without a doubt that God would not let that be the totality of this baby's existence, to be born and to die in that river. God must give all of us the opportunity to participate in the Trinity and the unity and in relationships. Somehow, since that day, I understand the reason for the Hindu belief in reincarnation. I have essentially been reincarnated in this life. I am now living the life of my youth. I am my former self, but better.

Death doesn't frighten me any longer. Death unites us with God. The drugs and hospitals and pain scare me; the process is frightening. Don't we all want to skip over the pain of Good Friday and go straight to the joy and wonder of Easter? Much as we would like that ability, it simply doesn't work that way. I am more aware of death now. I have been through surgeries, I have seen my mother die, and have performed my sister's funeral. My physical state is bringing me closer to death. And so it's likely that this kid stage may be the final stage—my "play stage." I have to leave myself open to the fact that the kind of death I am exposed to now may be physical death. And so, I catch myself going through the aches and pains of this third stage. I am like a kid in that I am clumsy and tired—like a teenager—and I get off balance sometimes. It's the awkward age of adolescence. The only thing is I am in my seventies!

Starting in 1997 and on through the present, my peripheral neuropathy has burst into poisonous bloom. My hands and feet are completely numb and often tingle with pain. I drop my fork or knife. I paw at the Eucharist during Communion. I have to concentrate to stand because my feet are unable to feel the ground. I alternately fight against and become resigned to my fate. As I struggle with my various maladies and symptoms of age, my friends all ask me "How are you? Are you feeling better?" My answer is, "I am terrible. I feel like dirt. It's bad." "Oh," they stammer, at a loss for words. They believe great health is the ideal. Life has become a search for happiness, and everyone wants quick and positive results. Well-wishers tell me that I should pray for a miracle cure, but I am not disposed to pray for a miracle. I will pursue the medicines and see the doctors, but I am not interested in a miracle.

Patient waiting brings tremendous growth. I would welcome questions more to the tune of "Is it getting worse? How are you coping? How do you make sense of it?" I make sense of it by understanding that suffering is not understandable, definable, or manageable. Suffering just is. I am coming more and more to the theory that everything just is. It just is. Now. Present tense. Sometimes it seems as if I have known three gods in my life. The truth, however, is that there have been three of me in my life—each allowed me to see different aspects of God. When we view God from different perspectives, we see different facets of God. We tend to make God in our own image and likeness. We can only see what we are capable of seeing. We can't see all of God at once, nor perfectly. So in our lives we see different small parts. In due course, we will see God's all.

Chapter 23
Reconciling—The Sacrament

Recently I was able to be with Maggie for a time. We reminisced about the days at Indiana University. She noted that looking back, it was as if I was a 13-year-old in the 40-year-old body, and she was a 34-year-old in a 25-year-old body. And we agreed it was a nice memory. She was curious about my emotional life today and I told her about Christine. I love being with Maggie, but I no longer want to be married to her. I just want to be her friend. And I think she would say the same. In a way, the same is to be said of Christine. Christine has told me that it is too bad we didn't meet when we were younger. But now we enjoy being together, sharing the time, meals and calm.

I am approaching the point where only a little sand is left in the hourglass. It feels great to have been able to journey back through this book and think it all through, sort it all out. I am fully satisfied: I did an interesting thing or two—many interesting things.

I still make efforts to stop this frustrating disease. In 1998, I went to Indianapolis to see a research doctor at Indiana University. After two days of using me as a class guinea pig, he discovered that my red blood cells were enlarged. This fact indicates that they are not circulating through the narrow capillaries of my hands and feet, he said. It is a form of anemia and he countered by putting me on massive doses of vitamin B1 and B6. It seemed promising at first, but the treatment didn't help much. I even tried a hypnotist to help the vitamins do their work. Before helping me visualize the B1 and B6 working in my blood and visualizing my blood cells as normal and healthy, he asked me, "Do you really want to be healed?" Well, yes, I did want to feel better.

On the other hand, I am learning so much from my state of imperfection and human frailties. I am not ready to throw this experience aside just yet. When I turn the illness into a spiritual journey, I see that I have learned to be patient and to let others do things for me. Nevertheless, every evening I sit in quiet meditation telling my red corpuscles that help is on the way and for them to be patient. It will all work out. I leave it to God as to whether I will get better or worse. The healthy prayer is a prayer for a miracle cure that ends with, "Thy will be done."

The infirmities are difficult, but educational for my spirit. In the late summer of 1998, I went on a weekend trip with a group of six priests—all friends of mine. They were so helpful to me. It killed me to accept their kindness, but I did. One morning, we were going out on a boat and I was hobbling down this steep grassy hill toward the lake. I was terrified of falling in front of my friends and embarrassing myself. But I got down there and got on the boat. It was a great afternoon.

Infirmity is terrible—especially because I have always been so concerned about what people think about me. Recently, after Sunday Mass, a man approached me to say that he almost came up at Communion to help me down the steps. And here I was thinking how well I'd been doing. I was really shocked that my condition and infirmity were that obvious. All I could say was, "Wow." I risk a lot by saying Mass for a congregation now; I suppose that's becoming obvious. I am still interested in growth and risk, though. Still, I do dumb things. For fun, I shock people—and even myself sometimes. For my seventy-third birthday, I went skydiving from a plane, piggyback, at 10,000 feet over Providenciales. Just another shot of adrenaline in these achy bones and numb feet. After I stopped worrying that my glasses were going to be sucked off my face, the jump was glorious. It's just the kid coming out, I guess.

I still enjoy the club camaraderie of seminary. In 1998, I began an initiative to get local priests to offer emotional support to our current bishop. Comrades, community, and the network of friends—I want to promote a diocese family spirit—the seminary, the church, the parish. Achieving a healthy, perhaps even intimate, relationship with our bishop is the cornerstone for accomplishing of our spiritual mission. Bishops have a terrible job in this era of fewer and fewer priests. It is a struggle to do the right thing and to hold it all together. And bishops cannot do it alone. Forty years ago, nine out of 10 priests would have said their goal was to become a bishop. By now, that has become a joke. No one wants that kind of responsibility any more. Being a bishop means dealing with endless complaints, endless staffing issues, endless worry. The only fun part is wearing the new vestments! I like the current officeholder in Evansville, Bishop Gettelfinger. I want him to succeed. He needs us and we need him.

We began a series of dinners and social functions between the priests and the bishop. It was good for us all. No shoptalk allowed. No complaints tolerated. Maybe the priests and the bishop learned to trust a little more. Or else, maybe I was just naïve. Proceeding from this belief, I still try to talk a little intimately with the bishop. I want to hear what his strategy is. I want to get to know him. The more time I spend among priests as an elder priest, the more I see real fear. "What if I do this?" "What if I do that?" "How can I risk this or that?" Many of my classmates fear aging. They choose not to retire because they have no idea what they would do with themselves if given any amount of time to reflect. So they all stay where it is safe, and kind of snipe at one another. In that kind of emotional climate, even a bishop is an easy mark.

Bishop Gettelfinger is doing the best he can; he is doing what he thinks is right. But priests in this day and age are not inclined to go looking for reasons to be sympathetic to a bishop. I have no doubt that many of them have misinterpreted Bishop Gettelfinger and for that reason they are not cutting him any slack when he seeks to fulfill his personal needs—needs that every priest must fulfill or risk becoming a statistic. It was the same for Bishop Shea. He was just trying to do the job right without enough self confidence. His fear of doing something wrong led him to govern, not lead. Unfortunately, there is no school for bishops; no course named "Diocese Management 101." You don't get a diploma you can wave around and say, "Look, I graduated! I got all A's! This proves I can do the job." They each muddle through it to find their way. All bishops intend to be compassionate shepherds, but that's not the way it often turns out. So bishops become CEOs, go to the public relations functions, and rarely get to spend time with any priest. They end up commanding rather than leading. Leadership through commands only entrenches opinions and makes change more risky.

The longer I live, though, the better I can wait. My insight is that "It ain't my church, it's God's—through Him, with Him, and

147

in Him." When I sought to be possessive of the Church in my youth, it drove me nuts. So I can wait and watch it unfold, but I still think we'd all be better off talking over a beer with our bishops.

As I waited for God to speak in the Church, God spoke to me by taking away the work on Provo. After two years on Providenciales, I was respectfully replaced by four priests from New Jersey who will be there full time. Bishop Burke was extremely kind, as he usually is, in handling the situation, and I was grateful for his effort to find me another Caribbean assignment. I decided to sit back and wait and let God reveal to me what I should be led to next. And I waited. But then I got impatient and decided to speed the process by pursuing an assignment to the Cayman Islands. I even flew down there to visit. They were interested, but never got back to me. I realized I was pushing God. So I waited again in Evansville, and soon I got a call—but it was from Arizona.

A small group of Sisters of St. Benedict requested that I consider being chaplain to their new monastery in Phoenix. I paused, changed direction and headed west, joining them in December, 1998. At the monastery, I had a chance to be quietly alone with God. Again I was able to experience the community of a Benedictine order—just as I experimented with one back in the 1940s at St. Meinrad. As I see the transcendent and contemplative God, I too become more transcendent, more contemplative—which is good. I can sit quietly and listen to the Lord and be process- rather than goal-oriented. That process of no action, of quiet prayer and listening and just being, is my preferred form of prayer now.

My time in Arizona lasted two years. I am now fully retired, going each year from friends in Florida at winter's end to friends in Evansville in summer. I intend to live until I am 85. That way, I at least know I have time to do some things. Having said that, I know that I am not in control, but I am allowing that there will be time for more. By allowing myself that space, I am more open to hearing whatever God is calling me to do. This stage—this third stage— is opening me up more to God's presence in my life, in my day. I don't have to do it all on my own. Looking back, this has been the most exciting life I can imagine. I have gone through my adolescence and learned about my feelings. I learned to be responsible,

148

to grow up, to be mature. I have had the chance to do it all often enough so that I can finally live out my life in a good, healthy way. Since my third life began, in Rockport in 1975, I have been getting progressively more comfortable with myself. I am filling in the missing pieces between my first two lives.

I seem to be living my life backwards because, as I mentioned earlier, I was never able to be a child (in the normal sense) when I actually was a child. In fact, I have never been allowed to be a child until recently. I didn't have a normal childhood. My father's death put me in a position of responsibility, of caretaking, because I was the oldest. I cut grass and did the chores, fixed the meals and babysat. Because I went to the seminary just after eighth grade, I never did the dating and hanging out that teenagers need to do. It was intriguing to go through it later.

There is always time for change. Growth, risk, and trust lead us to become a whole person—a holy person. I am beginning to feel as if I have become a whole person. I feel a certain new dynamic within me and I am not afraid. Well, I am still moderately afraid—maybe 40 percent of the time. All priests should have the opportunity and courage to test themselves the way I have. I have muddled through and managed to learn about love and God along the way. It is sad to see my friends stuck in their loneliness and adolescence. Perhaps they are unaware of it. Maybe for them the journey has been different. Somehow, I don't think so.

Not long ago, I was at a funeral dinner and sat at a table with several colleagues. A few of them began teasing one of our group about his "road women," asking if they had followed him as usual to his latest assignment. They were all laughing, teasing about his bunch of women—women who care very deeply for him. Even more telling was the fact that they unconsciously did it in a whisper, to keep the other tables from hearing that this priest had intimate friends. It is a telling statement when intimacy is a source of self-conscious giggling among a bunch of men in their late sixties. Intimacy is a joke, just as it would be to a table of barely adolescent boys—boys who like girls, but don't want their buddies to know it. Despite being treated as a joke, these relationships carry great responsibility. I have seen that in my varied experiences.

That incident took me back to my first life, where I used to convince myself it was all the woman's decision. In the late 1960s, with my "platonic" companions immediately before, and with my physical relationships immediately after Maggie, I took no responsibility. Instead, I acted all surprised and innocent when the relationships got too intense: "Oh, hell, you aren't getting serious are you?" These old men dining together after that funeral are me in my youth, wanting their kicks as well as having the protection of the collar to hide behind. It's admittedly tempting, and it's fully possible to never confront this desire to have it both ways. But hiding stunts you. It leaves you jaded. It hurts you.

Lately, I have risked reconciliation: I've put the sacrament on the line by speaking the words out loud to the persons I hurt. After 30 years, I called the cosmetologist, the woman I shared my first sexual affair with. I made up my mind to be reconciled. For years, the guilt had haunted me. At this latter stage of my life, I felt it was time to reopen this door. By apologizing for having hurting her, for using her, for my selfishness, I could let myself let go. I called, and she invited me to come on over. Opening the door to my knock— before I could utter a word—she said, "It is great to see you! You look great! Come on in." She had changed much in the intervening 30 years, as I know I have as well. She was thin, frail and worn. During lunch she shared that she had cancer and was in aggressive treatments. We chatted about the illness, her family, my current career moves. Light conversation.

Finally, I had to do what I had come there to do. The words just tumbled out of my mouth. "I abused you. I was a jerk. I am so sorry," I said. Without a pause she responded, "Well, I was a jerk too. I used you, too. It's OK. It's a good enough memory now." Then I asked for permission to write about her. She gave it readily. I was extremely touched by her generosity and kindness. Not long after this reconciliation, I looked up another woman I had used to fulfill my physical needs without regard for her emotions. As with my former lover the cosmetologist, this woman and I had shared rooms and secret trysts. She had shared emotion and I let her. She even went so far as to leave her religious order in hopes of us growing old together. I let her. But I never let her in.

150

Now she lives in Washington, DC, a successful book publisher. She, too, got married and found happiness. Still, I had to say the words. When in Washington recently, I called. She seemed to be glad and invited me by for a visit. Again I spewed forth an apology that comes from years of hidden guilt and fear. She said, "Hey, we were both adults. I had my free will, too. It's OK. It turned out to be good." It was good—good to speak about my sins, to be reconciled, to be forgiven. I am giving it all away now. I am unburdening.

With Maggie, Ann, and Christine, I never pursued the physical. We never took it that far. But the power of going all the way with our emotions changed my life. The unions were spiritual. I am not certain they were celibate. Because, I am not sure what the term really means. The intertwining struggles brought to me by women and celibacy have been the focus of my existence. When I look back at the bigger picture, I know that I have always been attracted to women. They, in return, have given me a gift of creativity, excitement, and risk, and have opened me to move beyond myself. I never really wanted to be celibate. What I wanted and what I continue to want are relationships that are nourishing and healthful. They don't have to be genital relationships, but they have to be genuinely intimate relationships that free me to go beyond, to be creative and to be myself.

I have always been drawn to women and most of my risk taking has been in relationships with women. I don't sense having taken too many risks in relationships with men. We have always been buddy-buddy about sports, common interests, and the like. In fact, my most intimate relationships with men have involved healthy discussion of our relationships with women.

Celibacy forces a person to spread out horizontally rather than vertically. When one marries, one deepens that relationship and that married relationship singularly colors the way one sees everything else. When one is celibate, it is a marriage to the Church and the Church becomes the vertical relationship. The Church colors the way one sees everything and everything is in relation to the partner—the Church. For better or worse, the Church has been my stable partner. I appreciate it now more than ever. Until now, I have never been much into this stability stuff. I have moved 34 times in my life. Three of those moves came before I was 15 years old. But I have become very comfortable with the Catholic Church. It is a big, strong umbrella, and although I am far over on the dripline, I am still part of it. And proud to be so.

Yet I am still looking. I ask God daily, "What it is that I am supposed to do?" I am still seeking what's down the road. And what of the vow of celibacy? Does it mean forever? Well, I don't know. I just made it again this morning.

AMEN.

Epilogue

During the winter and summer of 2001, and finally the early spring of 2002, for nearly two years, Jim approached his death. Congestive heart failure. Maybe he was all used up. Maybe he was enjoying the process. Or maybe he was still trying to teach me something, to let go slowly. Anyhow, that's what happened. I learned something about the process, about selfishness, letting go and worry. I also learned that optimism only gets one—even Jim—so far.

But mostly I learned that life and death are OK. Each is a process. It's OK to die, before the book deal, before the end of someone else's particular story.

He died April 15, 2002, and was buried at St. Joseph Cemetery, Evansville, Indiana, in what we call the Priests' Circle with his brothers. It was very touching to read the names on those headstones and to know the stories about brother rivalries, infighting and the gentle, subtle masculine caring. Just a family after all.

It's good to note that just prior to his last illness, taking full advantage of a pacemaker installed in the fall of 2001, Jim took a tremendous journey to Harbour Island. I understand he had a great, even excessive time, with friends, food and pink sand beaches. Even though the trip likely hastened his death, he went out full throttle. Like he said, 100 percent of anything is not a good thing.

Jim is still teaching me how to look at life and how to live it. I encourage you to take a risk of weakness, of assuming you don't know everything about your faith or your life. Most especially take the risk of getting to know a Catholic priest, a nun or a religious brother very well—intimately. They have a story to tell.

Ann M. Ennis
May, 2002